A tale of two horses

Hubble & Hattie

A passion for free will teaching

Kathie Gregory

Kathie Gregory

freewillteaching

Chapter 1
Present day

It's the end of December.

I would love to say that the land is still covered in a soft layer of fluffy white snow, sparkling in the morning sun, but, alas, this is North Devon: the snow has gone and it is raining. Again.

My husband, Matt, and I live on a small farm raising a limited number of rare breeds for sale. There are cows, pigs, sheep, chickens and ducks to keep us busy. Along with the farm we have a few other activities on the go: Matt writes bespoke software, and solves people's computer problems. When not engaged in these activities, he is an electrician and a musician, teaching clarinet and saxophone. I am an animal behaviourist, artist, and art teacher, as well as duty accounts and invoicing clerk for all our enterprises.

Back when Matt and I first met, we could never have imagined we would end up where we are. We had always wanted to live in the country with lots of space; even entertaining ideas of, perhaps, being a little self-sufficient. The reality is even better than we could have imagined. We eat our own meat, our chickens and ducks provide our eggs, and we grow our own fruit and vegetables. Well, apart from last year when nothing much grew at all! Matt makes sausages, burgers, gammon and bacon from our meat ... he made some brilliant pork pies and scotch eggs the other month. The only problem is that I haven't found a way of earning enough money to keep him in the kitchen rather than out at work! Probably just as well, otherwise I would spend all my time running around the fields to stay slim!

Our home.

Being self-sufficient benefits us and the animals –
some of this is for the pigs!

We must save a fortune not having to buy certain items from the supermarket, and they taste wonderful. Whenever people stay with us the first question they ask is: "What's in the freezer?" and the second: "What are you cooking for dinner?" And I thought they were staying for the pleasure of our company!

We have a small woodland, so use our own timber for barns, fencing, and whatever else needs mending or making on the farm. It's so quiet and peaceful, you could go a good week without seeing anyone. The isolation is not everyone's cup of tea, of course, but it suits us very well.

The farm is run on the basis of everything having an influence on everything else. We do things as naturally as we can to help the land, so that produce and animals complement each other and thrive. Companion planting, cross grazing, understanding the relationship between nature and the environment as a whole helps us to work in ways that maintain the balance. This philosophy is very important to me and everything I do is from this perspective.

This summer has been one of the wettest on record and the fields here are totally waterlogged.

And what of the animals?

The cows are thoroughly fed up; their feet are a rather unattractive mud-brown colour, that sink well into what is now a good six inches of churned mud, with not a blade of grass in sight. They are, however, very adept at finding places to shelter from the wind and rain when they become bored from standing in their field shelter.

The chickens spend more time in their house than out pecking, which is fair enough. Even their feet sink into the horribly soft, gloopy mud.

The pigs have gone to sleep. If all else fails you can count on pigs to have a good nap, although it's good to be aware that, as pigs get depressed fairly easily, sleeping is a non-coping strategy. Having things for them to do when the ground is bad and they can't get around much is one way of avoiding this. Everyone says pigs love mud – and they do – but only up to a point!

Meet our farm animals: introducing Strawberry and Ruby ...

... the chickens ...

... Pudding, one of our pigs ...

A tale of two horses

... our flock of Hebridean ewes.

Our sheep are coping well. Small, woolly and black, our little Hebrideans are not at all challenged by the weather. Without grass, they eat the hedgerow, which seems to be far tastier than the hay we put down for them. Hay does make a nice bed, it seems, however: not exactly what we intended, but there we go.

This time of year is the busiest on the farm, but the quietest for everything else. All the animals need feeding twice a day, and, if the temperature drops and the mains water pipes freeze, they also require water taking to them in buckets. It is quite easy to spend an entire day thawing – or trying to thaw – frozen water pipes. Carrying enough water for all of the animals is a serious challenge, and we do not have that many compared to larger farms. Do you know how much water a cow drinks in one sip? A whole bucketfull! They seem to drink much quicker than the horses: one giant slurp and it's gone! As the days are short, everything has to be done before it gets dark, and trying to move water about the farm in the pitch black is even harder!

Fortunately, at this time of the year people have other priorities, such as Christmas, so our other work slows, and even stops altogether if we have snow. You have to go uphill in every direction from here, which is just impossible with ice- and snow-covered lanes. As a result, we regard December and part of January as an enforced holiday from our other activities, and just concentrate on the farm.

This is also the time when, unfortunately, I have to sort out my advertising for the coming year. In rural areas such as ours, the main type of printed advertising material is the parish newsletter, inclusion in which means your advert must be ready to submit by December, and will then run in a year's issues of the magazine. I have two weaknesses: one is marketing; the other is technology. So, my first headache is working out what to put in my advert to attract people; I honestly have no idea, other than saying exactly what it is I do. At least, this way, there are no misconceptions – but it doesn't make for a very inspiring advert. My second headache is working with the software programme, Word. It's just as well I only have to type to write this book, otherwise it might not have been done ...

What is it with Word changing things all the time? You select a font and size, and apply it to the whole document. It should follow, then, that everything you type will be in the font and size you've chosen – yes? No! Every time I change the layout, by adding or removing a line, Word 'helpfully' presents the words I have moved in a new, 'interesting' font and size that bears no resemblance to that I had chosen. Sometimes, it even changes the font colour, and places the sentence at the start of the line, rather than centred. Why? I really wish I knew! Matt says that this is 'predictive text,' but I can tell you that what Word comes up with is not in any way, shape or form predicting what I want! The only thing that can be predicted with any certainty is that I will curse and ask Matt to sort it out!

Each of our work activities needs advertising, so this ends up being quite a lengthy and frustrating process. Oh well, at least when it's done that's it for another year. Now I only have to worry about how effective the adverts will be. You can see how annoying I find this: I am supposed to be writing about horses and I've been sidetracked!

Introducing the horses

So, on to the horses, Charlie and Star: strong and hardy; sweet-natured and happy. I love their strength and size: Charlie has really good, thick bones and long, rangy legs with big, strong muscles, despite being retired for the last few years. Star is more elegant and graceful, but just as strong and capable. The sense of power and ability that can be discerned from looking at them is amazing, and seeing them play and gallop is just magical. They are so inspiring; I could watch them all day.

My horses are calm, reliable, and predictable in their behaviour. They make happy, contented, 'purring' sounds throughout the day. I often hear them purring to themselves; it sounds like

And here's Charlie, my big, strong boy ... (Courtesy Andy Francis)

*...and Star, my truly beautiful girl.
(Courtesy Andy Francis)*

enthusiastic sighs! They come to help whenever we are on the field, and usually wander along with us as we walk Indie (our dog). They are pretty enthusiastic about everything: breakfast, play, and laying in the sun. Not that there's much sun in December, but they both have an afternoon nap, still.

We often have 'Mum and horses' time in the afternoons or evenings. Star likes her mane being combed and I am happy to oblige as it's really nice and relaxing for us both. Charlie likes a head rub and nuzzle, which is just lovely, too.

Re-evaluating self

As for me, I have come to realise that life is too short to waste and that the support of friends is extremely important. I'm not a very sociable person: I don't find socialising easy, and don't know what to say most of the time. Asking for help just makes me feel insecure; I always wonder why somebody would *want* to help me. But as I've developed and gained confidence by working with Charlie and Star, I have found myself able to open up to people, and not be so insular.

Knowing people who can tell me when my worries are unfounded or over the top also prevents me from deciding that an idea is not a good one, and giving up on it. There's a real tendency to let my worries get out of proportion; to become obstacles I simply can't get past. The thought of what might go wrong is invariably much worse than the reality, of course, but, when gripped by worries, I don't see that.

I have spent the last few years carrying out four or five different work activities, whilst telling myself that I multi-task because I would be bored with a single job, but this is only partly true. The main reason is fear of failure: a huge stumbling block I can't seem to get past. My reasoning seems to be that if I am too busy to pursue any one thing to its conclusion, then I cannot be considered unsuccessful at it. You can't fault the logic, but you certainly can fault the way that this attitude restricts me, and prevents me doing or achieving what I want to. Why shouldn't I be successful if I put in the work

and make it happen? Success is not only for other people, I can experience it, too.

A couple of people who have seen Charlie and Star have suggested that I have a lot of knowledge and information to share, and that I should write about what I've done, and how I've achieved what I have with them. They say it's obvious how much care and passion I have for what I'm doing, and how kindly I treat the horses: there are others who will want to hear about my methods, and who will be encouraged to try them for themselves, they say. Of course, the thought of doing this just makes my insecurities kick in again. What have *I* got to offer?

I know deep down that how I work with Charlie and Star is right. I use only kind and compassionate, positive reinforcement methods that achieve results without compromising my animals' physical or psychological well-being. I do not have any doubt about that at all. I do still have doubts and insecurities about my abilities, however. Writing about my experiences is a nice idea, but can I really see myself doing it?

After a lot of soul-searching, I share my thoughts with Matt. The reality is that I rush around trying to get everything done, with not quite enough time for all of it – actually a really rather stressful situation. I teach art, aerobics, and dog training classes; I take on behavioural assessments, and do the accounts for local companies. I do the invoicing for Matt's electrical and software work, the banking for everything we do; the accounts for all these things, too. I design websites for each activity: leaflets, business cards and adverts for local magazines. I run the house and the farm pretty much on my own as Matt has to do the day job to keep us afloat. I teach the horses, walk and play with Indie; cook the dinner.

I have discovered that it is much simpler to have my shopping delivered, as I don't have time to fit that in, too. Things like taking the companion animals to the vet for vaccinations, or getting the car fixed are almost impossible to manage without significant rearrangements to my diary. In winter the

A tale of two horses

situation is worse, as I have commitments to the people I teach or provide services for, but still have to manage all of the jobs on the farm and at home, which makes me decidedly frazzled. The days are so short I barely have time to get everything done. I rarely eat as there isn't time, and I am constantly trying to catch up and not be late. Added to this, when I look at how much I earn against how much time I spend getting to the various places of work – petrol costs, advertising costs, and any legal requirements such as licences or insurance – I am actually making a substantial loss! I am supposed to be contributing to our income, and on the surface it appears that I am, as I have lots of things on, but, in reality, I'm not. And there is no way that this will change, as I don't have time to do things properly, and develop any of the activities I undertake into a proper business. At the moment all I have is a handful of sidelines, which are making me stressed and costing me money.

Matt and I agree that my assessment of the current situation is accurate and not sustainable.

So where do I go from here ...?

FOLLOWING MY DREAM

I know that I don't enjoy all of the things I do, and the work that provides the most potential for growth and a career is animal behaviour; what I like doing best.

This is where my future lies. Charlie and Star have shown me that. I am very good at this. I may not be confident enough to shout it out (yet), but that doesn't change the fact that this is what I do best.

Matt agrees with my decision to drop everything else and work only on this: this clearly necessitates lunch! An odd thing to say, you might think, but we have found that we get so much more done if we go out to lunch and do our planning then. Someone gave us this great piece of advice years ago, and ever since we have been going to lunch to assess where we are and plan the future whenever we have difficult decisions to make. If we stay at home we talk about it for a bit, lose track, and then can't be bothered.

So lunch it is.

I've been musing a lot about what has been said about my horses, and I think there is a story in chronicling our first year, and how I went from receiving the most surprising birthday present ever to where I am now. Matt thinks that detailing my experiences in a book is also a great idea. We eat and think, and a plan emerges.

I hand in my notice for several of the jobs I've been doing, and also tell those who come to my aerobics classes that I will finish at the end of the year, just a few weeks away. As animal behaviour is to be my main activity, I will concentrate on writing my book.

I must start addressing things, and stop sticking my head in the sand when something seems scary or difficult. I must be brave and not let my insecurities overtake me, because, if they do, I might as well not start on this path, as it will all be for nothing. I have to admit, I'm finding this all rather surreal. I feel like I am about to live someone else's life. Can this really be me? Can I really make a go of it? What if it doesn't work? I refuse to go back down that particular, dead-end road. If I don't try, I'll regret it. I feel that, just maybe, I can do this ...

MISCONCEPTIONS

Back to the main attractions – Charlie and Star – who are happy and content; really enjoying their new home and life. At the moment, they are spending more time in the barn than out in the field, but when the rain stops or the sun is shining, off they go for a wander and graze. Oh, and also a roll in the mud ... hmmm, and just when their hair was looking so clean and shiny, too.

Their diet is mainly hay in the barn, grass when they wander outside, and a helping of Speedi-Beet® at breakfast – one of their favourite things; they come running when I shout 'breakfast' across the field!

The barn is 30x30ft (9x9m), and a completely open space with no stalls. One side is kept permanently open, and goes straight onto the yard, which then opens onto their field. Charlie and Star are free to come and go as they please, twenty four hours a day. Barefoot, their feet are coping well, despite the extraordinarily wet weather. Their hooves are strong, with a lovely, compact shape developing nicely. They have really thick winter hair, rivalling that of any Exmoor pony! They had their summer lightweight, zero tog rugs on for a couple of days in the spring, when it was hideously wet and windy, but, since then, have only had the same summer rugs on for the week this month we had snow. Their nice, expensive, heavyweight winter rugs have gone unused, and remain packaged, ready for next year, should the temperatures drop enough for them to actually feel cold. Their relationship with one another is going from strength to strength, and they are both so much more confident in themselves than when they arrived.

Given how I have described the two, if you had to guess which breed Charlie and Star are, you might be thinking along the lines of a hardy native breed: perhaps a Welsh Cob, or Irish Draught Horse. In fact, they are none of the breeds that we consider hardy, but Thoroughbreds and ex-racers, with behavioural problems to boot! This begs the question: why are they so hardy, strong, and good-tempered when the general perception of their breed is so very different?

Exclamations of horror for taking on Thoroughbreds as my first horses were followed by various snippets of information and advice, all of which were concerning, and not at all reassuring. Some of the descriptions of the Thoroughbred temperament I have heard over the years, from people with experience of them, are that they are –

* Highly strung
* Flighty, and nervous at best
* Completely mad
* Aggressive
* Nasty
* Horrible
* Unhandleable
* A danger to ride

One person even described them as totally insane, and another claimed that they kill foals!

Regarding their physical constitution, they are claimed to be weak with thin hair and skin; not hardy; prone to injury and illness; requiring a whole range of rugs for every weather and temperature. They are said to suffer from the effects of flies, so require fly masks, and dislike both heat and cold. They have very bad feet (it's said); are unable to go without shoes, and need special diets, vitamins and minerals.

Wow! This is certainly not a recommendation for the breed, and would, in fact, probably deter most people from owning one; I was told that not even experienced horse people and professionals will take them on if they don't have to. It may surprise you to learn, therefore, that, contrary to popular belief, Thoroughbreds are not one of the weakest, least capable breeds, but are actually of native hardy origin.

Thoroughbred ancestry can be traced back to three foundation stallions: the Byerley Turk, the Darley Arabian (foaled in Syria), and the Godolphin Arabian (foaled in Yemen), all named after their owners: Captain Robert Byerley, Thomas Darley, and Lord Godolphin. These three animals were amongst over two hundred oriental horses brought to England during the seventeenth and eighteenth centuries, and are regarded as foundation stallions, as all modern Thoroughbreds descend from them. They are also the only ones who continue to have direct male descendants.

Bred to native sprint mares, the offspring were the first of the Thoroughbred breed. Selective breeding concentrated on using only those horses who excelled on the racetrack, developing the breed into what it is today. This method of selective breeding is still used, suitable sires and dams being chosen after proving themselves on the racetrack.

THOROUGHBRED CHARACTERISTICS

A refined nose, and long, sleek neck sit on a strong, deep chest. The shoulders are well sloped and muscular. The withers are high, with strong hindquarters and long, straight legs. Standing at

A tale of two horses

an average of 16 hands, Thoroughbreds come in a variety of colours: black, grey, bay, and chestnut. Many have white markings on the face and legs. Roan colouring is rarely seen. They are truly elegant examples of the horse.

Originally, Thoroughbreds were used in endurance tests as mature horses of over four years of age. Match racing was the main discipline; races were run in heats, over distances of up to four miles. As racing evolved – with courses becoming shorter – breeding focused on producing horses who were faster over these shorter distances, and able to race at the younger ages of two- and three-years-old.

Nowadays, they race from two-years-old, the length of their career depending on their success. As they grow older, not unnaturally, they tend to become slower, with youngsters having the edge where speed is concerned, although not experience. Retirement can be at any age, depending on the horse and his strengths.

Increasingly, ex-racers are finding their way into companion or competition homes, with many competing to high standards in a number of disciplines.

Thoroughbreds are very fast, spirited animals, often described as highly-strung, or nervous. In the racing environment, that temperament trait determines their behaviour. Tall and elegant, these horses have evolved to become as efficient as possible to aid speed, and bred to exploit a heightened flight instinct, making them one of the fastest.

It is for these reasons that making the transition to a new home can prove difficult for many ex-racers and their new owners, and when Charlie and Star arrived with us in January, this was certainly true of them.

This is the story of our first year together ...

Chapter 2
Dream? What dream?

I didn't really want horses; I mean I really *did not* want them. I didn't, for example, dream about owning one, read about them, gaze longingly at any horse I saw, or think how lucky those who had one were. However, my husband and my mum disagree with this perspective. *They* say that I have always wanted horses, and they know this because I have consistently said so. Hmmm ... that's not how I remember it.

I once *did* want horses – when I was ten years old. I loved them then, read books and bought magazines about them, and even knew how many I wanted, and what colour they would be. That particular summer, a friend down the road offered to give the ten-year-old me a lift to her riding stables, as we didn't own a car, and, for three glorious months, I rode horses, although, alas, this was the beginning and end of what might have turned into a lifelong enthusiasm. As I grew up, there was not much opportunity to ride: other things took priority, and I thought less and less about horses.

I met my husband, Matt, when I was twenty one, and we set about earning a living and making a life for ourselves: a life that did not include horses; nor did it ever intend to. We went on the occasional hack when on holiday, but that was about it. As far as I was concerned, I had archived any dream and longing for horses years ago. I have inherited my father's logic, and knew that, short of winning the lottery (somewhat unlikely), I had no chance of ever owning a horse. I therefore did not waste energy and thought on something that was not going to happen.

However, although I was under the impression that, for the last twenty years, I had successfully put away my dream of ever owning a horse, apparently, everyone else knew that this was not the case! And now the dream is a reality. I have horses, and, from the moment they arrived, the part of me that I felt was missing is now here; I am complete.

Nothing about my life thus far has in any way been to do with working towards owning horses. My first job was applying designs to kitchen and bathroom tiles. It was great. On my own in a little room within a big warehouse, I loved being my own boss and deciding how to organise each day's work. I was responsible for all aspects of my job, from start to finish: organising the orders, selecting the tiles, designing patterns and applying designs, firing them in the kiln, checking that they all came out to the same high standard, and packaging and labelling them ready for customers to collect. Working on my own – and the artistic element that the role involved – made this job ideal for me.

After my design work I had a series of manual jobs, including bar work, shop work, and shifts at a petrol station. It was all hard graft: long hours and low pay! Eventually, someone gave me a break and I got my first office job. What a relief it was to never again have to do back-to-back shifts!

I then pursued a career in finance, where the intention was to study and qualify as an accountant. This was about as far removed from horses as it's possible to be, so it's no wonder that I didn't exactly

A tale of two horses

grab this career with both hands! I had pink hair, a loathing of blouses and skirts, and preferred my own company, so perhaps office work was not a well thought-out option. Indeed, I was just going along with an opportunity that had arisen, due to a lack of anything better. Although I've always loved animals, at no point did it occur to me that, maybe, just maybe, this was where my future lay. I became bored very quickly, and moved jobs often, soon working on a temporary basis as a troubleshooter. This helped alleviate the boredom, but the constraints of office hours – and fitting into that environment – told me that this was not the career path for me.

The beginnings of a new career

By this time, Matt and I had become the proud owners of two cats, Cracker and Snowflake. Although I didn't grow up with cats, I knew – or, rather, thought I did – why our cats behaved the way they did. I seemed to have an answer for every question Matt asked. Why does Cracker keep trying to sit on Snowflake? Why did Snowflake pounce on my feet? What on earth are they doing now? It took a while for me to realise that I had a strong empathy with our two cats, and was – albeit unknowingly – analysing their behaviour. Matt suggested that, as I seemed to know a lot about our cats' ways, perhaps I should find out if I was right? Wanting to know more about animal behaviour as a result of this, I read all the books I could find, which confirmed that my opinions were correct, and I did indeed know what was going on in my cats' heads. I researched courses on this topic, and the rest, as they say, is history.

I have now been involved with animals for over fifteen years, working holistically with them, and understanding that a change in one area of their lives will affect everything else. I did my training with The Centre of Applied Pet Ethology (COAPE), and was tutored by Professor Peter Neville and the rest of the team. What rang true for me was the organisation's philosophy: to truly understand animals it is necessary to look at everything that

Cracker and Snowflake – my interest in animal behaviour started with these two cats.

has an impact on their behaviour, including the environment and the emotional state of the animal; not simply their general behaviour patterns. Instantly, I knew this was what I had been looking for; what I believed in.

COAPE courses teach ethology (the scientific study of animal behaviour in the natural environment), as well as how to understand the emotional aspect which motivates and affects behaviour. Most animals we meet in everyday situations will not be living wild in their natural environment, of course, so it is vital that we understand what they would be doing in this situation, and what effect their changed circumstances have on their natural behaviour and emotional state.

Many people dismiss emotional states of mind as irrelevant, but we must acknowledge the fact that emotion is an intrinsic part of cognitive awareness, which holds the key to understanding an animal's motivation. To me, it seems logical and obvious that studying emotional make-up should be integral to behavioural studies and training. Without an in-depth understanding, a connection with and understanding of animal behaviour is not possible.

How I work

My approach assesses the genetic, emotional, motivational and reinforcement aspects of behaviour, alongside the instinctual and physiological needs of the animal. All of these facets have an impact on an animal's underlying emotional state, mood, and expressed behaviour, and ultimately affects their ability to cope in any given situation, and also how they interact with people and other animals. Once we understand why animals behave as they do, we can make changes to how we work and live with them, and how we communicate. Moreover, we can provide an environment that ensures their emotional and physical well-being.

The resultant environment benefits both the animals and those working and living with them, allowing identification and use of the most ethical, effective, and productive methods of doing so, which should, in turn, reduce the severity of, or even put a stop to, any behavioural issues. From this point it is easy to progress to teaching alternative, acceptable behaviours and coping strategies for those animals who, like us, need help dealing with what life throws at them.

THE BENEFITS OF POSITIVE REINFORCEMENT

As far as applying these principles to equine care goes, giving my horses self-awareness and the ability to make decisions is invaluable. For example, if my horses are cold or wet they know to come into the barn, rather than zone out and stay where they are, but if they don't need to seek shelter, they won't. An aware horse who knows what to do in a situation, and what coping strategies he can fall back on should he need to, will be a more confident, balanced animal, whilst a horse who is incapable of looking after his own basic needs is not. If trained to understand that there is no threat in following his owner's wishes, and he does so willingly, an animal will become reliable, safe, and secure. But if forced into certain behaviours or actions, he will invariably panic if things go wrong, and be unable to decide for himself what action he should take to cope with a stressful situation.

Just as a horse should be able to provide for his basic needs, so, too, should he be able to manage his own behaviour, and know how to act in any given situation. Of course, he will not automatically know what we consider to be appropriate behaviour, and what responses we want him to give, but we can teach him to understand and appreciate that different situations call for different responses, providing him with the confidence necessary to react appropriately.

I do not teach helplessness; that doesn't get us anywhere, and certainly won't result in a horse who can manage himself. What it will result in is me doing everything for him, which is counter-productive. I have myself to manage; I don't need the added difficulty of having to manage a horse as well, when it is more beneficial to teach a perfectly capable animal to manage himself. If we are each responsible for ourselves, we can concentrate on working together to achieve a better understanding, and more mutually empathetic relationship. This partnership develops our ability to increase our awareness of each other, and assess situations and respond together to achieve mutual goals.

The journey that Charlie, Star and I have shared has not been easy, emotionally, and I have found it rewarding and difficult in equal measure. It's unrealistic to expect every new horse owner to work through all of the problems and behaviours that are seen in horses with behavioural issues without some help, as many will simply not know how to effectively resolve these issues and situations, and could even make them worse. However, there are a number of steps, based on knowledge and understanding, that could empower an owner to make an educated assessment.

I hope that my book helps increase your understanding of horse behaviour, and inspires you to develop a stronger relationship with your horse, or any other animal in your care, by encouraging a change in your perception of handling and training, and to question whether the established and widely-used current methods are the best way forward. I will show you that there *is* a better way of working with horses, using a thorough and properly-scientific approach to our understanding of behaviour to improve our skills and techniques, to the benefit of our equine friends, and ourselves.

My methods are based on positive techniques and bonding, which, when applied, will allow a true partnership with your horse, founded on mutual trust and companionship.

Chapter 3

Life begins at 40

It's January 2012, and I have just turned 40, the age when life begins, they say. Did I really expect my life to change today? No. It's only one day on from yesterday – not very different – but I obviously did not anticipate my husband's determination that my life *should* change so drastically when I reached 40.

And the reason? A horse. Well, *two* horses to be exact, and they are all mine.

My wonderful husband had decided that I could not pass this milestone birthday without a horse, so he bought me one ... er, two. It was a 'buy one, get one free' deal ... I was thrilled.

However, in the heads of my friends alarm bells began to ring ... I'd never owned a horse; I hadn't even regularly ridden one. And, my concerned friends were quick to point out, the horses in question were Thoroughbreds; ex-racers: not exactly the most sensible choice for a first-time owner. And they had 'issues.'

I wasn't brought up around horses, so my hands-on experiences are precious few. My friends concluded I had no idea what I was doing, was completely mad, and it would all end very, very badly.

CHARLIE AND STAR

Let me introduce you to those horses, Charlie and Star, whose arrival in my life was a complete surprise.

Charlie is a teddy bear of a horse, with big, strong muscles covered in short, thick hair. He's a wonderfully dark bay, which does mean that he's invisible most of the time as he blends into the background, and I'm forever scanning the field trying to spot him. It's easier in the summer when the trees are in leaf, and he stands out better. He has small ears and such a loving face.

Star is perfect. A gorgeous, dark dappled grey, she's like a supermodel with long, long legs, and the very skinny body of a recently-retired racer. She is also very beautiful, with the longest ears I've ever seen. I reckon she could pilot herself very well if she took off!

Charlie had a successful racing career, and was put out to grass when he retired at six years old. He had been rehomed a couple of times – the longest for a year – but each time he was returned as it didn't work out. He was described as 'lovely and sweet, and you can do anything with him,' so he was offered as a companion for Star.

Star stopped racing at three-and-a-half years old. She was tipped to *be* a star, win every race, and have a great racing career, but she couldn't cope with the environment. I was told she was faster than the horses she was trained with, but when in a race situation, the noise, unfamiliar horses, the jockey's efforts at increasing her speed, along with her insecure personality, made her slow and retreat in a race. It was clear she was not going to achieve her potential, so she was withdrawn from racing.

She was also a nightmare in the yard, and difficult to manage; I got the impression that it was a relief to see her go, although she was well-liked in general.

My husband bought her and she arrived at

her new home three months later, along with Charlie – the free one.

FIRST THOUGHTS

As an animal behaviourist, the first thing I did when they arrived was observe and assess my new charges. My professional opinion was that there was an awful lot of work to be done in order for them to become content and well-balanced horses.

Star had no confidence and was very scared.

sensible manner, and no awareness of her body. She was so clumsy! Her feet were fine if she was going in one direction very quickly, which she did, often, but other than that her legs were all over the place. She banged her head, her knees, her body. Oh dear, are we sure her eyes are working?

Charlie had decided that there was no point in living, and so barely reacted at all: the polar opposite of Star. His only reaction – when he did respond – was to bite. His coat and eyes were dull,

She was so reactive she would not stand still at all, and the moment she was touched anywhere she was off. She wouldn't stay in the same area as me, and if I even approached her she was gone. She hated grooming, water, touch, headcollars, and really, well, pretty much everything. There was no chance of her standing for her feet to be done: if you got near enough to touch her leg she was off again.

She had no idea how to move her feet in a

Star when she arrives: highly-strung and very skinny.

19

A tale of two horses

Charlie did not see much point in living, it seemed. when he arrived.

his apathy all-too-apparent in the way he simply stood with his head down, his body sagging. He also suffered from a skin condition, digestion issues, and sarcoids. His feet and teeth had not been properly tended for a long time. Both of the horses arrived barefoot, as shoes are often removed once the animals are no longer racing.

The horses were put together a week before I got them, and apparently ignored each other for that time, or, rather, Charlie kept Star at arm's length if she came too close. When they arrived with me, this situation had not changed: every time Star came near him, Charlie tried to bite her. Nevertheless, she continued to try and get close to him for reassurance (if he went out of sight she panicked), only for her insecurity to get the better of her and cause her to kick him! It was obvious that they did not have a relationship at that point, and were barely tolerating each other.

Clearly, behaviourally, there were so many issues to work through that this could not be a short-term project. I needed to address almost every aspect of their psychology, from the lack of

Star walks away the moment I go near her.

self awareness, conditioned responses, learned behaviour, and the relationship with each other, to their emotional states and responses.

My friends were not altogether wrong in their misgivings, as it turns out. A lot of the behaviour that Charlie and Star engaged in is often considered normal with Thoroughbred temperament. Thoroughbreds are often difficult – misunderstood – and can be reactive when they are moved from the racing environment to a completely unfamiliar one, where everything from handling, routine, and riding is different. If people take them on, set them straight to work, and expect them to understand the cues they use with other horses, things can go wrong: without time to adjust, they may not behave in the manner expected. Thoroughbreds are considered more spirited than those breeds noted for their quietness, but nature and nurture play a part in this, and what you see on the surface is usually only one facet of the personality that prevails.

So, although being mindful of breed characteristics is a good thing, being aware that there is much more to an individual horse is essential to helping him develop and grow. And my friends had not taken into account that animals are my profession. I had no intention of simply mounting up and riding Charlie and Star, as I don't work with any animal without first assessing where they are behaviourally and emotionally, which ensures I know what to do and how to act to keep us both safe. Once I know how things stand, I can decide on a plan going forward. And anyway, who better than an experienced behaviourist to take on the more difficult and behaviourally-challenged animals that many would find too testing ...?

BREED TRAITS
My plan? To resolve all of the issues that were causing my horses to be emotionally unbalanced; to take them back to neutral, and to start again so that their minds could develop and grow in a healthy way.

A little like resetting a computer to factory default after it has gone wrong so that the machine can start anew.

In the case of Thoroughbreds, the British Horseracing Authority works with and supports various organisations that assist in the welfare and rehabilitation of those animals who have come out of racing, so many get off to a good start after their racing career has ended, and any problems are quickly dealt with before they are rehomed. But many people do not go via these routes when they purchase a Thoroughbred, and often acquire a horse without any formal or well-thought-out rehabilitation or retraining. However, Thoroughbreds are only one breed, of course, and any horse might arrive at his new home with significant behavioural issues, and a lack of understanding through not having had appropriate training or development.

Advertisements from owners trying to 'move on' their Thoroughbreds are plentiful. If taken on without any appreciation of their psychological state, and what they have been taught and how they have lived, things will often go wrong, and their reputation for being difficult perpetuated. This fuels the idea that these horses are unmanageable, and that the average owner is, perhaps, ill-equipped to take one on. But is this really right?

Common breed traits can give an *idea* of

A tale of two horses

temperament, but this also depends on the individual horse. So what if Thoroughbreds are not naturally 'difficult'? What if their apparently unmanageable, highly-strung temperament is a result of their circumstances? Could they become good-natured, trustworthy horses? And what if we are making a huge mistake by writing off these wonderful creatures as useless and worthless?

There are plenty of examples of Thoroughbreds going on to compete at the highest levels in other disciplines after they have finished racing, but is that success only achievable by those at the top of their profession? Or could anyone work with the horses to achieve a well-balanced, reliable animal?

Perhaps, at this point, many of you are exclaiming that your Thoroughbred is wonderful, and what on earth am I talking about? Unfortunately, I believe that there are just as many – if not more – owners whose experience has been the exact opposite.

As previously mentioned, there is a huge misconception that, as a breed, Thoroughbreds are highly-strung, unmanageable, and aggressive, but if we take the time to consider what they have experienced in their lives, we can begin to understand why they often behave in this way. Their environment, the demands of racing, how they have been managed and trained to achieve racing success: all of these elements shape how they learn and their resultant temperament, plus how they respond to people and other horses. Bred to be as fast as possible, the racers are selected for speed, not their sweet nature, resulting in a temperament that is more reactive, and quicker to switch from thinking brain to instinct mode than other breeds, such as those who have been bred as drays, say. The Shire horse would not be capable of hauling heavy loads, ploughing fields, etc, if his flight instinct took precedence, and he was quick to take off if spooked by a strange noise or flapping object!

Ultimately, we are manipulating that flight instinct when we race Thoroughbreds, as without it they would not run as fast. By triggering this survival strategy, we make them run as if their life depended on it, reinforced by the environment in which they are placed. There is peer pressure, too, as other horses in the race also flee, the jockeys urging them to go faster with their whips, the noise of the crowd adding to the feeling of danger and urgency. Of course, it's not actually as straightforward as that because, if it were, the horses would be in a blind panic, truly running for their lives, the jockeys unable to guide them around the racecourse.

Much more goes on in a horse's brain than one base emotion or instinct; it would be a gross over-simplification to assume that this is the case. Horses can and do enjoy the disciplines for which we train and use them: after all, domestication began around four thousand years ago, and we have developed their cognitive abilities just as we have with dogs. They are not primitive animals with a limited ability to learn; they are much more advanced than this, which means they have great capacity for mental and physical stimulation.

CONSIDERING INSTINCTS

In any given environment, some horses will thrive and others will not. Horses who cope well and have a successful racing career can often be re-homed in a similarly competitive environment, and many go on to compete at a high level in different disciplines. The horses who come out of racing early for any reason other than injury are often those who do not have the temperament and disposition to cope with the demands of such an environment: they may be too reactive, their instincts may kick in too readily, or they may not have the necessary drive. In these instances, they are often re-homed as companion animals, or in a non-competitive environment.

Of course, there are Thoroughbreds – calm, sweet, reliable animals – who have adapted easily to their new environment and lifestyle, but there are also those who have reacted in a rather different and unbalanced way, with less than ideal results. Charlie and Star are Thoroughbreds, and this book is about them, so my behavioural analysis of the behaviours they have presented are from their perspective, but the concepts and principles I apply are the same for each and every animal. What is different are the personalities and experiences of each animal, which are responsible for the many expressions of behaviour we see, so understanding the horse you are working with gives you the ability to tailor and apply behavioural techniques for the individual. Often, people want to immediately ride the horse they have bought, which means the animal is put straight to work. In the case of racehorses, those with problems are usually emotionally stressed, and have well-established, learned responses to being handled, which may not best suit what is now being asked of them. As a result, the owner may use coercion, force or restraint in order to handle the horse.

When this happens, as far as the horse is concerned, he is still being asked to do something he perhaps does not want to, which makes him feel uncomfortable, so he continues to respond in the way he always has. And, of course, he is probably still only a youngster, without the experience to understand what is being asked of him. It's all too easy to forget – and some new owners may not even appreciate – that all of the training thus far has had the objective of training the horse to run as fast as he can in a straight line. Often, racers are mounted on the move, so cannot know that their new owner would like them to stand still whilst mounting. Widely-used rider aids – reins, body and leg control – do not necessarily transfer to a racehorse, as he may not understand what response is required: tightening the reins may mean 'slow down' to most horses, but to a racer, this means go faster!

Consequently, misunderstandings arise between new owner and horse, and trouble ensues in the form of reactivity, stubbornness, fear aggression, or unpredictability, giving rise to and endorsing the misconception that Thoroughbreds are quite mad and difficult to handle.

THE EMOTIONAL MIND

Armed with this knowledge, I feel well equipped to embark on this exciting journey with my horses, despite having almost no practical, hands-on experience. I know my profession, and I understand behaviour and learning theory very well. Of course, the science of behaviour is only half the picture, and many people miss the fact that it's necessary to understand the emotional mind as well. Horses are not machines, and they experience emotions just as we do: they can be happy or sad, and have likes and dislikes. Their emotional well-being is intrinsically linked to their overall temperament and behaviour, just as ours is.

The emotional mind is the most often overlooked aspect when training or working behaviourally. For some, it's simply a case of the horse understanding what he is supposed to do from a physical aspect: about a million miles away from truly understanding animal behaviour.

For example, imagine that a chemist learnt only how chemicals interact with each other, rather than what the effect would be if they were subjected to heat, cold, light, dark, different substances, receptacles, etc, etc, and what they do upon contact with a body. Only a partial understanding of the subject would be possible if this was the case. By ignoring the emotional mind and the psychological factors that influence behaviour, the same is true of working with animals, ultimately consigning any attempt to failure. If you cannot understand why an animal is behaving as he is, how can you know what to do to change it? Science has a long history of refusing to acknowledge that the emotional mind is an intrinsic part of why animals do what they do, but, more and more, it has become accepted that it is the driving force, the motivation, behind all animal behaviour – including our own.

Thankfully, nowadays, a more accepting approach to recognising that studying one aspect of the brain does not give us all the answers prevails. Neuroscientists, behaviourists and ethologists must work together if we are ever to fit together all of the pieces to the jigsaw that constitutes the mammalian brain, and see the whole picture.

Only then can we begin to fully understand how the mind works.

Chapter 4
Reality dawns

My initial thoughts: what exactly have I taken on, or rather, what exactly has my husband got me into now?

The last time that Matt did something impulsive and not at all sensible was when he bought our farm, which actually turned out to be the best decision he had ever made. However, I had grave misgivings at the beginning.

For a start, our property is a small, concrete bungalow with a limited lifespan. Then there's the space – or lack of, to be precise – it provides: a tiny, two-bedroom, one-bathroom abode, which is challenging on a daily basis! Most of our furniture is either piled up inside (which makes it very cluttered), in the garage, or has been sold. Anyone who has downsized will appreciate just how difficult it is, and we have gone from a six-bedroom, three-bathroom, three-storey house to this. That's the bit that had me worried.

The land, however, is a different thing entirely. Eighteen acres, with a four-acre woodland, it's exactly what we wanted, and our dogs love it: having their own fields to run about in, just outside the back door, is a dream come true, and even more so as our rescue dog, Coco, has problems with other dogs. Here, she can go off-lead, without fear of other dogs being around.

My insecurity shows

Now, it's all very well having dreams and imaginary scenarios about how life might be if I had horses, but the reality of being responsible for their health

Indie and Coco enjoy roaming the fields of our new home.

and happiness is very different. What if I can't do it? What if I've taken on too much? Am I out of my depth? Is there any truth to the perceived Thoroughbred reputation? Are they really highly-strung, unpredictable, evil horses who will run rings around me? As has been frequently pointed out to me, no one in their right mind would choose to take on one of these horses, let alone as a first horse. The horses will surely know that I have no idea what I am doing; will sense my weakness and be completely unmanageable. Not only that, I haven't made life easy for myself or Charlie and Star by taking on two ex-racehorses who didn't know each other until a week ago when they were put in a field together.

Not long after the pair arrive, Matt and I are walking in the adjoining field, with me exclaiming, yet again, at how wonderful they are, when they decide to tear about. Okay, so they're fast, I think to myself, now that I've seen them running – well, more like flying, really. Star goes from a standstill to about as fast as it is possible to in the space of a second or two. Wow!

"Er, are you actually going to get on and ride her?" asks Matt.

"Oh yes," I reply, enthusiastically, and, from Matt, unvoiced but loud and clear, nevertheless: "Oh God, what have I done; she'll kill herself."

Matt looks at Star galloping around the field at full pelt. He thinks it's scary; I think it's exhilarating and breathtakingly wonderful.

"Well, you'll be okay," I tell him, "Charlie's a bit slower."

Frankly, I don't think he finds this reassuring, but I've been on a fast horse before. Some years ago, a work colleague circulated an email to ask if anyone was interested in making up a group for a day's hack in the countryside. When I told Matt, he said "You like horses; let's do it."

I put down our names, and one cold, early autumn morning, a couple of weeks later, we drove to the stables, arriving to find a group of people dressed in stylish jodhpurs and riding jackets; hats and boots. I looked down at myself dressed in jeans, two jumpers, a sheepskin jacket and trainer-type boots, and then at Matt who was dressed much the same.

"I hope we're not with them," I whispered, "We'll look like complete idiots."

Naturally quite shy, standing out from the rest of the group is not likely to make me feel comfortable enough to strike up a conversation. I comforted myself with the thought that perhaps they were with another group ... or perhaps not, I realised, as I spotted a work colleague within the group. Although everyone was friendly and nice, they couldn't quite hide their incredulity that we had actually turned up wearing what we had; perhaps also wondering if we could actually ride, and had any idea about what to do. This was fair enough, I guess, as we certainly didn't look the part, plus, I'd actually only ridden twice since I was ten years old (though, thankfully, the others didn't know this!).

It seemed that the stable girls who were allocating horses to riders felt the same way, as Matt was given a very large and – it turned out – extremely slow horse. "Is he for me?" he asked: "Surely I'm not going to get on something that big?"

Unfortunately for Matt, the biggest horse on the yard was indeed for him. I could only sympathise – my poor husband is scared of horses!

It was my turn next.

"You'll like this one," the stable girl said. "His name's Jack, and he used to lead when racing. He was really fast. He's twenty one and blind in one eye, so he only goes slowly now."

Okay, thanks, I thought. Jack was very sweet, and somewhat smaller than Matt's horse.

With everyone mounted up (Matt had to climb a high set of steps to reach his saddle) we set off.

We had a lovely morning just walking with the occasional trot along lanes, across fields and streams. The scenery was stunning, and it was a lovely day. Actually, when I say 'we' had a lovely morning, I am referring only to myself. Jack needed no cue about where to go, it was a very familiar route for him, and all I had to do was enjoy being on a horse and outdoors. Matt, on the other hand, did not have such an easy time of it. It soon became apparent why his horse was considered slow: he clearly intended to eat every piece of vegetation along the route, taking Matt halfway up banks to get to choice leaves on out-of-reach trees, and heading off in a different direction in pursuit of a particularly tasty-looking morsel. More often than not, Matt's horse simply stopped and refused to move until he'd tasted everything he considered worthy of eating!

After lunch the guides gave us the choice

of a slow and shorter walking route back to the stables, or a longer, faster one that was only an option if we were capable of cantering, which posed another problem for Matt, as he has no sense of balance when on a horse (I've no idea why this is, as he actually has a really good sense of balance ordinarily: in his spare time he has raced dinghies and practised martial arts). However, it all seems to go to pot when on a horse.

It seemed sensible for Matt to choose the easier, slower route back, leaving me free to take the faster route with the majority of the group, a decision which prompted some raised eyebrows! There's more to horseriding than just experience, I believe: I may not have had many hours in the saddle, but I have always been completely comfortable on a horse, and have a wonderful sense of balance. (The same cannot be said for when I'm on the ground, sadly, as I bump into anything and everything, along with stumbling over my own feet.) I wasn't worried, and, in any case, Jack was old, half-blind, and slow.

Hmmm, perhaps someone should have told Jack that!

Our group walked and trotted for a while, and then the path opened up and we were on open ground. The horses obviously knew that this was where they could have a good canter as they began gaining speed. What a lovely sight: all of those well-dressed people looking really professional and at home in the saddle.

I'd established a really good level of communication with Jack throughout the ride, and, although he became excited when the others started to lengthen stride, he held back, awaiting my instruction. It felt so easy and comfortable, as if we were in tune with each other, so I let him have his head and off we went. What happened next was one of the best experiences I've ever had.

Jack took off at a smart pace, overtaking everyone else before they'd got up any real speed. His movement was so smooth and assured, I was happy to go with him and let him find his pace. We galloped across open land, the wind in our faces, totally together and having the most exciting time,

galloping all the way to rejoin the lanes that led back to the stables. We slowed, looked round, and saw the rest of the group in the distance! When they eventually caught up with us, they were full of congratulations and praise for me: "I've never seen anyone ride like that," someone said. I took this to be a positive comment; confirmation that I didn't look too ungainly! The praise from people who owned horses, rode regularly, and saw a lot of people riding suggested to me that, perhaps, I had missed my calling. I was being told that, actually, I was really, really good at this, even though, as far as I was concerned, I hadn't really done anything terribly spectacular!

The slow and fast routes had converged at one point, and Matt's group had seen us galloping. Back at the stables, the first thing Matt said to me was: "My God, do you know how fast you went?"

"Quite fast ..." I laughed, as I dismounted without looking too concerned, "... it was great!"

Returning to the conversation we were having whilst watching Star, I asked Matt: "Do you remember how fast Jack went when we had that day's riding?"

"Oh yes," he replied, "That's one of the reasons I thought Star was perfect for you."

"Oh, she is," I said, smiling to myself.

Out of my depth

One brilliant experience years ago, on a horse who used to race in some way, was, perhaps, an unrealistic basis on which to hang my hopes for Charlie and Star. Were my dreams achievable? Well, there was only one way to find out, although crossing your fingers and jumping blindly into something is never the most sensible approach, particularly if it is entirely different to anything ever experienced before. It certainly pays to do at least a little homework, to get some idea of what to expect, and how to plan to get where you want to be.

Turning a hobby or a dream into a business is not easy, and many new ventures fail in their first year, simply because the person taking it on is so far out of their depth that they are not aware of what is involved, or when to worry that things are not going well. Subsequently, they fail to make the adjustments necessary to preserve their dream.

With only three months' continuous experience of being around horses in a riding stable environment, and various isolated encounters, was I one of these out of my depth individuals, I wondered? I did ride bareback on some gypsy horses many years ago, and well remember the feeling of freedom and wonder that this gave. Riding was one thing, but the actual day-to-day management involved was something I'd not done, so I didn't even know about tack and clothing, for example: which saddle to use; which riding hat, stirrups, and body protector? Neither was I able to name all the parts of a horse, or how to motivate them to move and stop when I wanted. So many questions!

And don't get me started on headcollars: I can't even put my dog's harness on the right way round! Indie stands patiently as I try to work out which foot to put through the loop, and how to fasten the harness. How the hell am I going to work out which way round a headcollar goes? And even if I did manage to work it out, would the horses stand still long enough for me to put it on?

Not having a strong background in horses could be a serious impediment, or just might force me to think more laterally. I may not know the correct form, or how things are done, but I am also not set in my ways. Without preconceived ideas of how things 'should' be done, I would be forced to think 'outside the box' about how to achieve what I wanted to do, and in a way that benefited me and my horses. A win-win situation.

Have you ever been on one of these self-development or 'How to be more confident' courses? They teach you how to establish a win-win situation in order to increase your confidence and achieve your goals. A brilliant idea: they should teach this kind of thing in schools. If you haven't had the benefit of one of these enlightening courses, ask yourself this: 'How many times do I do something because I've always done it like that, or someone has told me

that this is how it must be done?' Sometimes, things are done a certain way because it is indeed the best way to do them, but this is not always the case, so it's important to take time out to assess whether what we are doing is being done in the best way it can be.

Starting a new job, most of us have probably been taught by other employees how to fulfil the role we have. If we question why something is done a certain way, the answer, frustratingly, is often "Because we've always done it that way!" If we are brave enough to suggest that this might not be the most efficient method, our ideas and suggestions for innovation can be met with resistance. It's natural to resist change: we are creatures of habit; we go to the same table in the café, sit in the same place on a bus, because these actions and routines are familiar and reassuring.

The reality is that our dislike of change spills over into every aspect of our lives, and probably accounts for many people never having a go at something new, changing their circumstances, or following their dreams. Generally, we do not challenge what is familiar ... but maybe we should.

How many opportunities have we missed simply by not interacting with life, or being capable of varying our routines? Many people do something different – maybe something small like walk a different route one day – and by doing create an opportunity. For some it's a case of being in the right place at the right time, and even small changes can lead to a more fulfilling, happy life. When we are more open to change, it allows us to seize and take advantage of opportunities that come our way.

Applying this philosophy to my situation, it appears that, what someone in my position should do is give up the two Thoroughbreds I've just been bought, and start instead with one horse: a nice, quiet cob who will be happy to do whatever I want him to, and not react when I get things wrong because of my lack of experience. But, you know what? I disagree. Too often we let others influence our actions; what we should think, and what we are capable of achieving, ultimately leaving us disappointed and with our dreams unfulfilled. It may

A tale of two horses

be that the adviser is projecting their own anxieties and lack of confidence: they wouldn't be able to do it, so why should you? I'm as guilty of this as anyone, and Matt is forever telling me to stop being negative when I am helping him around the farm. I know that my negative comments stem from the realisation that I am the one who can't do the job in question, rather than Matt.

PLANNING AHEAD

At this stage I realise I really need to make an accurate assessment of my capabilities.

Firstly, what are my weaknesses?

- The main one is that I have no equine background/experience: my work with animals has concentrated on cats, dogs and small furries.
- I don't know much equine terminology, and have a very limited knowledge of tack and equipment.
- I've never done all the usual, day-to-day jobs such as mucking out, bringing horses into or out of a stable, tacking up, picking their feet.
- Physically, too, I must know my limitations. I am not strong: I have a back injury and brittle bones. It's a practical consideration that I must be careful with my body.

And yet, all of these shortcomings are things I can learn to work around. They should never be a reason to forego my dream, to give up before I've even started. If you put your mind to something and work hard, you can achieve your dreams and change your life. Recognise your strengths and weaknesses. Start working to those strengths, and challenge yourself to learn the things you need to. Take small steps initially and build from there as your knowledge and confidence increase.

And talking of strengths, mine are –

- I'm a qualified animal behaviourist with many years' experience.
- I'm the kind of person who will find an answer if I don't know it.

Charlie appears calm now, but how will he react when I handle him? – after all, I have little hands-on experience. (Courtesy Andy Francis)

- I'm not afraid of hard work; neither am I afraid to ask for help.

These qualities will help me achieve success. Having an in-depth knowledge of animal behaviour and learning theory gives me the confidence to know I can do this, and do it well. Despite my obvious limitations, I am probably going into this with more awareness and knowledge than the average first-time horse owner, and not just from the usual perspectives of experience and knowledge. I understand animal behaviour, learning theory, motivation and reinforcement. I've been working for the last fifteen years with owners and their pets, and seven years ago I began working with our farm animals. I have a lack of extensive practical experience with horses, it's true, and, as what knowledge I do have is theoretical, I have a lot to learn in applying that knowledge to the practical aspects of horse ownership.

So, I have a good starting point, but do not assume I know it all by any means. To look at it another way, rather than being out of my depth, I am in my comfort zone in terms of interpreting the behaviour I see in an animal; teaching and shaping this using positive reinforcement training methods, and providing a lifestyle that minimises stress and disharmony, and encourages resting contentment. The great benefit of this is that a content horse is less reactive, and is able to learn much more easily than one who is stressed.

Conversely, I am out of my comfort zone when in close proximity to the horses, and doing things with them, as I don't know them yet. This is something I will have to learn. Does picking up their feet cause alarm, or is this fine? Do they stand if I put a rug on? What about the vet: how will they be if he needs to see them? Will they react suddenly to things they don't like, or will they give some sort of warning? How do they behave in scary situations? Do they kick or bite, or shut down and not respond?

I don't know any of the answers to these questions, and have been told more than once that this will allow the horses to run rings around me. The only way of successfully handling them is to know what I'm doing – which, of course, I don't – and have the confidence to show them 'who is boss.'

A BETTER WAY

But I prefer a different approach: I do not want a master-and-slave relationship, but one that has been built on trust and understanding. When taking on an animal, whether a youngster, pedigree, rescue case or oldie, we should take the time to learn about them before we become hands-on and get stuck in. A good relationship is the result of getting to know each other, it's as simple as that, and does not happen just because we know how to behave around that species generally. Each animal is an individual, just like us.

If we know how to handle a horse, we feel confident that we know what we are doing, and all will go to plan. Unfortunately, what is frequently not taken into account is whether or not the horse understands what is being asked of him, or even if he is emotionally and/or physically able to comply. If we ask for something that our horse is not in a position to give, our relationship may not develop well, and both owner and horse lose out, with possible injury (physical and psychological) to ourselves, and/or our horse.

Imagine how much more effective and satisfying it would be if we first took the time to get to know our horse. Rather than assume that he will know what it is we expect of him, and respond accordingly, it's better to regard everything we do as a learning experience between horse and human, starting slowly and gently, assessing each response our horse makes. Then we will know whether our horse is happy to stand for his feet to be done, or if he hates being groomed. And there's less chance of him biting us if we approach grooming slowly and focus on non-sensitive areas initially (which vary, depending on the horse), rather than start in with a thorough grooming regime, expecting him to stand quietly whilst we do this. Ignoring a horse's body language (and that of any animal, for that matter) and what he is trying to tell us is a recipe for disaster.

Remember: horses are not machines. If we get into our car and depress the accelerator, it goes. If we use the brake the vehicle stops. We are rather inclined to expect the same from our horses,

A tale of two horses

and if they don't respond in the way expected, we don't understand why, and try harder to achieve the response we want. This only leads to further problems, either at the time, when we feel we must use ever-increasing force, or later as the relationship deteriorates.

Tackling those things that our horse finds difficult or scary in a calm, reassuring, step-by-step manner, we can gradually improve the situation, and what has the potential to become a real battle or issue, actually loses steam and disappears. At the same time, hopefully, horse and human are developing their understanding of each other, and establishing a relationship built on trust.

THE BUSINESS PLAN

I'm afraid I can make no apologies for suggesting that now is a good time to make a business plan. Just saying the words 'business plan' strikes fear into the hearts of many: pages and pages of seemingly useless information, which you, as the person with the dream or idea, has to provide in order for what you propose to work. Even worse, most of this information is unknown to you at this point. What will your annual turnover be? Who are your customers? Where will you be in five years' time? I have to confess it does seem rather a waste of time to try and provide the answers to questions that you cannot possibly know until you have started. There are so many possibilities and scenarios it's almost impossible to decide on a strategy.

Anxieties about writing a business plan are more than valid. I wonder how many business plans have been assessed, deemed viable, and financially backed only to find, in reality, that the business does not follow this path after all. No-one can predict the future, but your business plan needs to be as accurate as you can make it, whilst still allowing for adjustments along the way. With that in mind, a business plan is a useful and productive tool.

At present I am at point A. I have these wonderful horses, the first step towards where I want to be. I can imagine what it will be like when they are well balanced, happy and healthy. We will do all sorts of events, win prizes; people will say how wonderfully calm and attentive they are. I will take my career in this direction, and will have many horses that I have rehabilitated and found homes for, along with a substantial client base of people I have helped with their horses. This is point B.

There's just one problem: how the hell do I get there?

Ahh, of course! With my business plan!

Ignoring the finer points and financial aspects of the plan for a moment, and concentrating on the broader scale, I can use the strengths and weaknesses I have already identified in myself to form the basis of the plan. If I start with what I can already do, then progress each additional necessary skill to where it needs to be and what needs to be in place at any given point, I should have a clear path from A to B. It doesn't mean that I have to stick to this, or that it is set in stone, but at least it provides a clear direction, and highlights the goals I need to achieve. This is the future, not the past, so anything could happen, but with a plan I have something to inspire me, to look forward to, and tasks to complete. Without this, there's a chance that, in five years' time, I will still only be dreaming about how things might be ...

So now I have a plan, and the first step is to provide an environment for my horses that minimises stress and encourages resting contentment. There is no point in trying to work with a stressed horse, and making their environment as good as it can be minimises the negative emotions that adversely impact learning and training. Without actually doing anything directly with the horses I will have made them better able to learn and to listen; be less reactive and less anxious. This means that Charlie and Star will be more content, secure, and relaxed, and many steps in front of where a lot of horses are at the start, making my job so much easier.

Chapter 5
The plan

For any animal to be emotionally and physically sound, a habitat that will provide the freedom to express natural behaviour is essential.

In the case of horses, this will be an environment that is large enough to sustain their dietary requirements, provide motivation to roam, and ability to flee, but we routinely confine them in areas that are not big enough to satisfy these needs. In the wild, horses live outdoors in herds, not in a stable. We may keep just one horse or several but, generally speaking, each animal lives alone in their own stable.

The equine species has developed to be grazing animals, which they do for up to 90 per cent of the time. As owners, we provide concentrated feeds as an alternative to grazing, which are consumed very quickly. A wild horse is not encumbered by the weight of someone on his back, or wear equipment of any kind when in his natural environment, and there is nothing more unnatural to a horse than being ridden or hooked up to machinery to work.

When part of a herd, a wild horse moves freely about his environment, but still within the herd. But what do we do? We take individual horses out of the safety and security of their herd and ride, compete, or work with them, sometimes in unfamiliar places.

These are flight animals, who, if scared or threatened, will run away from the perceived danger, yet we routinely ask that they stand next to, or move past things that their instincts tell them are a threat.

From the foregoing, we can easily appreciate that what we ask of our equine friends is often the exact opposite of what is natural to them, and it's testament to the horse's ability to adapt to our needs that an equine-human relationship exists at all! Horses work with us, despite the fact that we may ask them to do things that go against every instinct; it's little wonder that, sometimes, they do not cope with this very well.

For an animal – or human, for that matter – 'resting contentment' is the overall emotional state that every well-balanced and stress-free creature should enjoy. This is partly achieved by living in an environment that satisfies physical needs: access to food, water and shelter in a form that is natural to the species concerned.

For example, consider an imaginary scenario of keeping a horse in a stable for 24 hours a day. We can meet his nutritional needs by feeding roughage and concentrated feed, and providing fresh water, and he also benefits from the shelter a stable will provide. Technically, his physical needs have been met, but in a very simplified, mechanical way. The real key to assessing whether or not the needs of the animal are being adequately met is the sentence, 'in a form that is natural to the species concerned.'

Horses are designed to graze, and, as already noted, they do so for extended periods. Anyone observing grazing horses will notice that they roam as they graze, and often quite some distance. So although we may be satisfying a permanently stabled animal's nutritional needs by

Horses are designed to roam as they graze.

controlled feeding, this does not allow him to express natural behaviour by movement or the way that he eats. Horses have evolved to behave in certain ways, but how we keep them, and the demands we make of them, often prevent them from doing so.

The end result? Suppressed emotion that converts to stress, and an attempt by the horse to carry out some sort of behaviour as compensation (known as displacement activities).

We talk a great deal about the stress that we undergo, generally short-lived nervous tension that we experience at certain times in our lives: when moving house or getting married, say. We can live with this type of stress, as once the event or situation that caused this is over, the stress subsides. The more damaging type of stress is chronic stress. Ask anyone going about their usual daily lives whether they are stressed, and they will probably say they're not. But how many of us have been in a relationship or job that is not right for us, yet have continued with it, even though we may know it's not good for us. Until we have been in this situation for a long time

and have developed serious stress issues, we don't tend to recognise that we are constantly stressed. It is this habitual, chronic stress which sits in the background that has a much more detrimental effect on our physical and emotional well-being.

Going back to our imaginary permanently stabled horse, he will not be suffering from the acute stress that arises from a specific event, but the chronic variety that is the result of an ongoing, stressful situation, such as not being able to perform natural behaviours, resulting in an attempt to remedy this. Box-walking and wind-sucking are examples of the displacement activities mentioned earlier, which a horse will resort to if unable to do what comes naturally. Of course, he may be displaying these behaviours for other reasons, too, but stress can certainly be a contributory factor.

The body's immune system is compromised when exposed to chronic stress: aches and pains seem worse, chronic conditions can become more symptomatic, and lethargy or reactivity can increase. Not surprisingly, this has an adverse impact on the emotional well-being of our stabled horse, and, if he doesn't feel well, he is more likely to respond with negative behaviours such as irritability, apathy, anger, or stubbornness. Stress also has an impact on learning ability. If our horse feels physically well and emotionally content, he can focus attention on learning what we are training and teaching him. If he is not in optimum condition, his mind will wander and not be as focused, which has an effect on how much information his brain receives and processes.

What effect on his stress level might turning out our imaginary stabled horse into a more natural environment have? As his stress level drops, he is likely to become more content as his needs and instincts are met, and he is able to perform natural behaviours, which will also positively impact his physical well-being and emotional state, making him more relaxed – in a more responsive mood state – and therefore easier to work with.

Think about the other aspects involved with how we keep our horses, and the things we ask them to do, and apply this same strategy. Even if your setup is not ideal and has limitations, there are always improvements or changes that can be made to ease anxiety and stress.

I have all this in mind when I begin.

Charlie's and Star's new home.

THE MOST EXCITING DAY OF MY LIFE

The horses have arrived; this has to be the most fantastic day of my life. I've gone through the day in a daze. Is it a dream? Sneaking out while Matt makes dinner, I look in the barn and there they are: it's not a dream; they're real, with hooves and manes and tails and everything! It's fair to say that Charlie and Star look as dazed as me!

Their new home is one large barn on a five-and-a-half acre field. Long-suffering hubby Matt has been busy these last few weeks, fencing off a yard area in front of the barn, and splitting the field into two: the top half as a summer field and the bottom as a winter field, both with a gate onto the yard. As the top half is wetter and more exposed, it should cope well with their hooves in the summer when the weather is dry, and the wind will keep flies to a minimum. The bottom half is harder and not as wet, as well as less exposed to the wind: perfect for the wet winter months. The gates opening onto the yard mean I can close each field for the off-season to let it recover. The barn is about 30x30ft (9x9m), open-plan with a supporting post in the middle, and one side left open so that Charlie and Star can come and go as they please, giving them the space to comfortably move around, and also for me to put hay at several locations.

Charlie and Star spend the first few days settling in: well, cautiously watching a black, furry thing at the end of the field, to be more precise. "What the hell is that, and why is it there? Better not turn our backs; it might eat us!" The black, furry thing in question is William our Hebridean ram. A very sweet boy who lost his mum when he was very young, so we hand-reared him. Not your typical ram in terms of behaviour, though – he's not very territorial about his environment, and, in fact, likes you to come in and give him a cuddle, which makes his tail wag! He comes when we call his name, and prefers company to being on his own. He is a herd animal, after all.

The horses however, are not convinced by William: he's clearly up to something. They remain vigilant and keep watch.

A tale of two horses

William, our Hebridean ram.

It's day three, and so far neither horse is very comfortable entering the barn. The moment they hear a noise or we get too close, they're off back out. They are coming in to eat, but are not yet convinced that the confines of the barn aren't providing cover for predators who may ambush them. They are much better outside, which is natural, as here they have the freedom to flee, should this happen (under threat, horses will take flight first, and only resort to defending themselves if cornered). At the moment their nice, comfortable barn represents somewhere that is difficult to escape from, so staying near the entrance, and going out into the open field when they hear something they're not comfortable with, is perfectly natural behaviour.

Our perception of the setup we've provided (warm, dry, and with food) is, of course, quite different. Why on earth would they be spooked? The instinct to 'help' them become comfortable with it, by enticing them inside, is the wrong thing to do in this instance. The horses do not know me or their new home, so any attempts will arouse suspicion or create anxiety about the barn, and/or me, and I don't want them to associate either of these negative emotions with me or the barn. No, the best thing to do is not worry about it, and carry on as normal.

As I have no idea how to pick out the horses' feet, and am nervous about putting on and taking off their rugs, I need some guidance and support, so have asked a friend for help. I also need to know how Charlie and Star are to handle, so Sue is giving me a hand. Her (not my) first job is to put on their headcollars, and then we lead the horses across the yard to the gate. Sue has a wealth of horse experience, so works comfortably around them, telling me what to do.

The pair arrived here with rugs on, but I've indulged them and myself and bought them nice new heavy-duty ones to keep out the cold, as they don't have much hair. Sue shows me how to undo the existing rugs, remove them, and put on the new ones. Okay, that's quite straightforward, I should be able to manage that. Charlie and Star look very smart: rugged-up to their ears, toasty and warm against the chill.

Next, we have a look at their feet. The pair stand quietly, although I do notice some small signs of anxiety – a little shuffling of feet and swishing of tails – though, all in all, it goes very well; they don't seem to be mad, highly-strung creatures at all!

However, it's all very well their standing for someone who knows what to do, like Sue, but what about me, who's not at all sure what to do yet ...?

I am in no rush to progress too quickly, as they may not be able to cope. Much better to let matters develop naturally without any drama, so I muck out, put down hay, talk to them, and generally do things around but not with them.

I am pretty much hands-off at this stage; so go the next few weeks.

Establishing a routine is the most important thing at the moment; the first step to creating an environment that my animals will feel safe in. Knowing when they can expect things to happen helps them relax, and quells the need to be on the alert all the time: an objective that will take some time to establish, but a very worthwhile step. However, at this stage there are a few things to be mindful of.

THE IMPORTANCE OF ROUTINES

If your routine is accurate to the nearest minute, your horse will work out the timing of it, and any lateness on your part can cause him to become frustrated, as he anticipates the event. If he is unable to resolve that frustration – either by way of a coping strategy so that it dissipates, or by it escalating to the point where it must be expressed by action of some sort, you may find him 'crowding' you, and trying to get at his feed whilst you are carrying it to him. If this behaviour progresses, it could become aggression (usually in the form of a bite) directed towards you.

I want my horses to learn the routine and know when things happen, but not to the minute, so usually work with around an hour's leeway for all routine activities. For example, in the winter when there is not enough grass, their first serving of hay is usually given at about 8am, although, depending on what else we are doing, may be earlier or later. This fits in with the rest of the farm, and means I can have a lie-in at the weekend, as the horses will not be standing at the gate waiting for their breakfast.

Frustration can also occur when your horse anticipates specific things that are very rewarding, but which either don't happen on a regular basis, or are a high point of the day (mine have a daily ration of Speedi-Beet®, which they absolutely love). Unable to manage the anticipation of such a nice thing, the same sort of negative behaviours can occur.

Self-restraint is what any animal practices if they wait patiently for a highly-prized reward, but it takes time to teach this concept. Self-restraint does come naturally to some extent – all animals understand the need to wait at some level, without having been taught it. Developing an animal's self-restraint and teaching him how to be calm and not become frustrated is a very valuable skill.

Charlie and Star have not shown a great deal of self-restraint, so this is something I need to teach them.

Star finds it more difficult to wait, so gets the bucket of feed first. As we progress and they come to realise that they will each always get a bucket of food, they will begin to relax about the situation,

and I can then work on boosting Star's self-restraint, with the end result that I can feed either horse first, without them following me around, shooing each other away, or trying to eat from both buckets!

Although talking about management in this instance, the same principles apply when working with your horse. Expressions of frustration and anticipation are common when something that is important to the horse is involved, and this may be a positive thing – such as food – or a negative thing – such as doing something they're not keen on, like, say, not wanting to accept the bit, being hacked out alone; even being groomed in some cases. Interestingly, in many of the cat behaviour cases I see there is little or no routine in place, due to the general idea that dogs need a routine and cats don't. All of us need routine in order to feel secure, whether living in the wild, or as a domesticated animal. Some species struggle more with change, and individuals, regardless of species traits, can be more or less sensitive to this.

A salient point to remember is that, whilst you are creating a routine, your horses are learning it, so it's important to be flexible in terms of what you expect. For example, if I expect Charlie and Star to come in from the field and stand exactly where I want them to every time, I am setting us up to fail. Consistency and reliability are things I can expect once they have become used to these notions, but until then I need to lower my expectations, and work towards that goal. And even when they do learn these characteristics, expecting the same response every time is not realistic. I know I keep saying this, but horses are not machines and will not behave as such. They have emotions, which will play a big part in how they act and respond at any given time.

OUR FIRST FEW WEEKS

It's six weeks in and I am still in a state of shock that I actually have real, live horses! Matt gets a daily update on everything they have done – whether or not he wants it – and our evening conversation usually starts with the now immortal words "My horses …" Fortunately, he is very pleased that I am

A tale of two horses

Charlie and William developing a friendship.

so thrilled, and is happy for me to chatter on – for a while, at least!

Although still very early days, Charlie and Star are settling in well; working out the relationship between them, as well as becoming familiar with us. Remember William, our Hebridean ram? Charlie seems to have struck up a bit of a friendship with him, and they are often seen nuzzling each other. Star, on the other hand, is still not convinced and tries to move Charlie away, prompting William to move – and Star to startle!

The time has come to get their hooves trimmed. Both are barefoot, and I have no idea whether the condition of their feet is good or bad. Enter barefoot hoof trimmer Clive, and his wife, Jill, who helps him. They spend time saying 'hello' to the horses, and then begin to work on their feet. Neither horse has great feet at the moment, it transpires, but there are no major problems; they just need time to develop and for someone to trim them well.

I am so nervous, I am positively shaking. Not properly knowing Charlie and Star, I've no idea how they will react to this treatment, an uncertainty that is not conducive to feeling confident in this situation. But the horses do well – they have had this done before, after all. Both now have better-looking

feet, and my job is to ensure there are no problems between trims.

Their rugs also need to go on and off as the weather warms up, and to check they are fine underneath them. I am not very comfortable with the clips that secure the straps, and envisage struggling with them, taking so long that the horses become bored and wander off, leaving me to sort rugs that are half on and half off! My default setting in a situation such as this is to ask Matt to do what I don't feel able to do myself ... but these are *my* horses, not his, and I need to be able to handle them, as how else am I going to do anything with them? I can't rely on Matt to do this for me every time, however scared I feel about doing it myself. It's not fair on him, and I want to be able to confidently handle my own horses.

For the first time in my life I actually want to get the better of my feelings of insecurity, and am determined to show Matt and myself that he didn't make a mistake when he bought Charlie and Star: I *can* work with them.

So, it's time to be brave, only I'm not feeling brave at all, just terrified, imagining everything that could go wrong, and worrying about what to do if it does. I was terrified when they had their feet done, and I didn't even have to do anything! My being like this is why Matt tells me to shut up or go away when I'm helping him on the farm.

I *have* to do this. With my heart banging painfully in my chest, and breathing fast, I go over to the horses. My hands are shaking so much it takes a while to undo the clasps, but the horses, bless them, stand there whilst I turn an easy task into something much more complicated. But the rugs are off, and I breathe a huge sigh of relief, and try to calm myself. I am boiling hot and covered in sweat. No wonder I usually choose to stay in my comfort zone, feeling this way is not nice! This seems like a small victory – I've actually done this on my own. Matt will be very impressed.

Putting the rugs back on Charlie and Star is even worse, but, once again, I manage it, and Matt is indeed suitably impressed.

Insecurity and self-doubt are quite often fuelled by the thought that we do not know what will happen in a situation that is unpredictable, and the resultant fear we experience prevents us being able to plan how to deal with it.

Over the next few weeks I become more comfortable with taking off and putting on my horses' rugs, but these jobs still make my heart pound. Not yet knowing how reliable Charlie and Star can be – whether they will always stand still for the rugs to go on or come off, or be more unpredictable in how they behave, is unnerving. My rational brain says "Leave it; wait until Matt is here so he can help" but I stop this train of thought as quickly as I can, or I will give in and wait for help, when I must be strong and get over my fear.

And it's not even as though the horses are a problem, they look at me as if to say, "Oh, mum, you've got it wrong again," and wait patiently whilst I put matters right.

I have been told on many occasions that if I show fear, my horses will pick up on it and run rings around me. Well, I am terrified on a daily basis at

Warm and toasty in their new rugs – what a relief I managed to do up the clasps!

A tale of two horses

the moment; my fear is so strong, they've probably picked up on it before I'm anywhere near them! Yet they haven't been difficult, or tried to take advantage of it.

LEARNING CHARLIE'S AND STAR'S RESPONSES

Thankfully, as I get to know what Charlie and Star do when I rug and un-rug them, I become less worried and my confidence increases. The thought that they may yet react in an unexpected way still makes me a little fearful, however.

Things are going well, and Charlie and Star are beginning to respond to me, and appear less on edge. I continue to develop a sense of safety and reliability in their environment, aware that I need to begin handling them a little, having been almost completely hands-off the last few weeks, other than a littl stroke or two.

Beginning with the basics – grooming and picking up feet – I soon discover that neither of them, for different reasons, is very keen on being handled ...

Not a good start.

Being young and insecure, Star's default response to anything and everything is to walk away very quickly; Charlie has learnt that his best strategy is to bite if I get too close. Based on those responses, the most likely outcome of my persisting with trying to do something with them that they do not want to do is that I will fail, reinforcing the notion that their response is the correct one.

Of course, both horses were fine when handled by my friend, Sue, just after they arrived, and when they had their first hoof trim, but this was because they were still unsure of themselves and their surroundings, then, and not confident enough to express their true feelings.

Their reaction tells me quite clearly what my next step should be.

My philosophy is based on free will teaching – my horses must voluntarily choose to do what I ask them to, and if they don't, it's up to me to find a way of teaching them to want to without using force, fear, pain, punishment or negative methods. (I am, again,

frequently told that this is another unrealistic dream which I haven't a chance of achieving.)

As you can imagine, as a result, I have learnt to keep my ideas to myself: negative comments about my way of working will only undermine my confidence and make me doubt myself. I've been told that, given a choice, Charlie and Star will not do what I want them to; I should demand the correct response from them immediately, a concept that implies it will be necessary to use corrective measures as a next stage if they do not do what I ask for the first time.

Where did the idea come from that a horse should respond immediately and correctly the first time he's asked for or to do something? This does not take into account whether or not he has understood what is being asked of him, or even if he is capable of complying. Have we lost all understanding of the concept of learning? Horses are not mind readers, and if they don't understand what is being asked of them because the instruction is not clear, how can they be expected to do it? How *could* they know how to respond in these circumstances?

Another important benefit of free will teaching is that I will have a calmer, more reliable horse if he has chosen to do something, rather than feel he has no option. There will be no battle of wills, so his emotions will be positive, balanced, and well within his comfort zone, promoting the calmness and self-confidence he needs to do as asked. When a horse chooses and therefore empowers himself in this way, fear, unease, and anxiety will not be present, which means he is less likely to perceive the situation as unpleasant, or a threat, and trigger his flight or fight mechanism.

Also, most crucially, a horse who feels free to choose will receive positive reinforcement from the action, making it more familiar, secure and normal the next time he is asked to do it. If I deal with Charlie and Star in a negative and forceful way, they are not going to learn in the same way, and will not benefit anywhere near as much, as if I work in a positive way.

THE USE OF PUNISHMENT

And there is another consideration that warrants a mention, even though it may not be experienced: some horses are still handled in such a way that it is technically torture.

Were you aware, I wonder, that the methods used to torture people are scientifically backed up, and are not simply random acts of violence and cruelty? (I promise I am not being melodramatic, here.) 'Torture' describes a very specific act, but you must remember that it actually has different levels, and can range from mild to extreme.

Three steps are involved in the successful torture of a victim –

- Pain: The obvious one, although the next two are crucial also.
- Control: The victim's ability to control their situation is denied.
- Predictability: The victim's ability to predict when things will happen to them is removed.

The more severe the pain, the more the victim suffers, and if he is unable to escape the pain, he has neither choice nor control of the situation. Not knowing when the pain will occur makes the situation horribly unpredictable, leaving the victim without defence of any kind, in a constant state of fear. The mind cannot survive intact in these circumstances; long-term psychological and physiological damage is the result.

So what does this have to do with our horses?

You may be surprised – shocked, even – to learn that the torture strategy I have described is a common and normal part of many horse training strategies, and, apart from the obvious point that this is undoubtedly an unkind way to treat an animal, it also causes an emotional impact that must be considered. A horse who experiences pain as a corrective measure, or who is not sure whether it is permissible for him to express himself, or if he should only do what is asked, is going to be unsure, and anxious about his actions, leading him to give

up offering behaviour of any kind, with training then grinding to a halt as the horse is not willing to engage with his trainer. There is also the knock-on effect of stress and the physiological disadvantages this has (as discussed earlier).

A horse who is comfortable offering possible solutions to what is asked of him is going to learn much better and quicker than a horse who is fearful of his training sessions.

STRATEGIES THAT WILL LAST

Thinking through training strategies allows us to understand these from the animal's perspective, and whether or not what we *think* we are teaching is what he is actually learning.

Our Great Dane, Indie, is considerably heavier than me. If I tried to pull him about and he didn't want to go, do you think I could get him moving? Not a chance! So what on earth possesses people to think they have the strength to move a horse who does not want to be moved? We must acknowledge the fact that they simply weigh too much to push, and if they don't want to move, they won't. In many instances, of course, when pushed, a horse will move as he has been taught to yield to pressure, but this is not always the case, and if we try this strategy with a horse who has not been taught to yield to pressure, we may get a very different outcome to the one we thought we were teaching, as he may learn to resist as soon as he feels pressure on him. He may also learn that doing something with a human is quite horrible, so perhaps he won't be caught in the first place.

Regarding teaching as an ongoing assessment of checking that what I am teaching is the same as what the animal is learning, and adjusting as necessary, means I can achieve the desired response, without the difficulties.

When Indie was a tiny puppy at nine weeks old (well, not that tiny, actually!) his training was based on the free will approach, with him doing what I asked, and not me doing it for him. Some things took a little more time to learn, and sessions weren't always without difficulties, but it was the best thing I

A tale of two horses

Indie as a puppy. It's never too early to begin training.

This scenario reminds me of our first dog, Konan, a Karabash – Turkey's national breed – a real challenge and such a character. The Karabash is a herd-guarding breed that has been developed to live with and protect the flock or herd from wild predators. The dogs work without instruction, and so have evolved to make their own decisions. Compared to other, popular breeds, they have not been over-developed for the show ring, or to live as pets, as yet. The majority are working dogs and their characteristics reflect that, with instincts and breed focus very much at the forefront of their behaviour. There are few breeders in England, as they are not pet dogs in the usual sense of the word, and therefore require homes where their needs are met, with owners who understand their behaviour. They are clearly not for the faint-hearted, or the unprepared.

Training is not as effective with a dog who is used to making his own decisions, and does not see the benefits of listening to you! I used to take a book with me when we went out for a walk, not because I was bored of my surroundings or my puppy, Konan, but because, sometimes, we would get so far and he would simply refuse to continue. Being quite happy where he was, he did not see a reason to move. The easy and obvious answer to his intractability, of course, was to pick him up and carry him: after all, he didn't weigh that much at twelve weeks old, and doing so would facilitate a very quick and easy solution (until he weighed too much for me to lift him, that is). But what would that teach him? Certainly not to continue the walk of his own volition.

So the book came with us and, when Konan got bored of sitting, we would carry on. Obviously, it was then necessary to prevent this becoming an established routine (I did not want to spend all of my walks standing around reading), so rewarding him when he did move gave him the motivation to do the same next time, and also gave him renewed interest in me. I then began to add in games and interesting activities, and, soon enough, he was enjoying himself far too much to sit about, refusing to budge.

Incidentally, Konan achieved Kennel Club

could have done, as Indie is practically perfect, and has continued to learn and develop, with us working together to achieve a positive outcome.

Too many dog owners tell me that their dog misbehaves, and gets into trouble all the time. When I ask what they've done to correct this, the answer is 'nothing,' 'scold him,' or 'shut him out.' They are missing the point. If the owners don't teach their dog how he should behave instead, he's probably not going to stop doing what they don't want him to, is he?

Konan making his own entertainment – dogs can find many ways of getting into trouble if left to their own devices!

certificates for obedience training, took part in agility classes, and raised money for Children In Need by performing forty three sit-ups in one session! Sit-ups are a neat trick where the dog starts off in a down position, and then moves his front paws backward so that he changes to a sitting position, achieved by asking for a 'down,' then a 'sit-up' etc. A lot of dogs really enjoy this exercise, and find it quite exciting, though maybe it's not the most natural movement for a horse! Some horses can manage quite amazing tricks, so who knows what Charlie and Star might be capable of ...?

Konan taking a well-earned break from performing sit-ups to raise money for Children in Need.

Chapter 6
Now what do I do?

It's now spring, and I am still smiling like the cat who got the cream! My horses are perfect and I love them to bits. Matt still has to listen to me talk horse at him: there's so much to talk about, this could go on for a while – poor man! Worryingly, the first thing he says to me when I've been out visiting or socialising is "Tell me you didn't talk horse at them?" "I did!" I reply, delightedly! I just can't help it: once I start thinking about Charlie and Star, my lips twitch and I begin to smile, wider and wider, until I probably resemble a mad woman, grinning to herself!

The horses are beginning to get to know each other better, and are not so reactive. Charlie no longer tries to bite Star every time she comes near him, which is a definite improvement, although Star is still very nervous and insecure – if Charlie goes out of sight she panics. But she'll get there: developing self-confidence takes time.

They both look really well: shiny coats; bright eyes. Star has put on some weight (she was very thin), and Charlie now has toned muscles and is a big, strong-looking boy.

Both horses are beginning to regard the barn as a safe place, as they do us, now, too. We're spending time with them and, if they get spooked, they run towards us rather than randomly race about. This is really good, positive progress. However, feed times are still unsettled, with neither animal happy to eat next to the other, competition over who gets hay first, and the breakfast bucket of Speedi-Beet® can only be put down if Charlie and Star are not standing too close, or they compete for that, too. Horses don't

Star and Charlie becoming friendly, and learning to trust one another. (Courtesy Andy Francis)

Getting to know who else lives on the farm ... (Courtesy Andy Francis)

automatically understand the concept of sharing; that they will both be fed if they wait their turn. Horses *do* share resources, but if it has not been established who eats where, when, or the resource is particularly enticing, or of limited availability, they are more likely to compete for it, with the successful horse denying the other access to it.

This competitiveness is another example of their lack of self-restraint, and not understanding that there is no need to compete for and defend the resource. Thankfully, it is quite easy to teach them that the other horse being close by does not pose a threat, and that they can both eat in a relatively small area without the need to protect and guard their food.

I continue with the strategy of teaching self-restraint discussed earlier by going first to the animal who is least able to wait – Star – gradually building her ability to manage her frustration and anticipation so that she is comfortable with waiting, and does not feel compelled to get at the food immediately. I also want to change her focus so that she is not associating me with her feelings of frustration, and I am not the recipient of whatever action she takes when she can't cope.

To divert her focus from me, I start by dropping a small amount of hay at her feet when she comes over to me. This engages her attention as she eats, and stops her crowding me as I walk, and place the hay in the usual eating place. Once she's finished this small amount, she can move to the pile of hay I've put down, with most of her attention focussed on this. In time, Star will realise that her food source is reliable, and will become less insistent on having it immediately.

As for the Speedi-Beet®, I make sure both horses are occupied eating hay at different locations before I walk in with the buckets, taking their bucket to them before they have a chance to decide they need to come and collect it themselves!

Along with this work with Star, I am also teaching Charlie to go to a different hay pile to Star's. If they can learn to be around each other at mealtimes – but not too close – they can relax and will not feel the need to defend their allocation. This, in turn, will help develop their relationship, and create a closer bond. The eventual outcome I expect is two horses who can move about the barn without the need for any defensive posturing; eat from the same hay pile, if they wish to, and do not feel the need to shoo each other away, or control the other's movements or access to food. I should also be able to come and go in the barn with both horses patiently waiting for me to place their hay without them crowding me, competing with each other, or needing to get to it before I've had chance to do this. Being able to give either of them the Speedi-Beet® first, whilst the other waits and does not try to steal the portion just dished, will further develop their self-restraint.

RELIABILITY: KEY TO GAINING TRUST

I've spent the last three months teaching them that I am always the same: calm, reliable, and predictable. I do not go from being soft with them one day, to frustrated and shouting at them the next. This is the first step in gaining their trust. I know there are a lot of first steps at the moment, and there's another one coming up next, but they are all essential to long-term success.

The next step is teaching Charlie and Star self-awareness, so that they can understand what is going on, and make appropriate decisions based on this. A horse with this ability is much easier to work with ordinarily, and far easier to calm and regain control of if things go wrong.

At this point, if my horses do not want to do something, they don't do it. Star is still unable to cope with being handled, and will walk away when I try to do anything with her. Now, I could have started from day one by putting her headcollar on, tying her to the fence (safely, of course), and handling

her anyway: after all, she'd soon get used to it, wouldn't she? Well, maybe she would have and maybe she wouldn't, but if she didn't, I would have a horse who was difficult to handle and who wouldn't keep still. Worst of all, the experience would have been traumatic for both of us, and even possibly dangerous. By using this method, Star's emotional state for accepting being handled will be one of fear and anxiety: she is submitting to being handled because she has no choice. And, as time goes on, one of two things will be likely to happen: she will become more reactive, or she will become more subdued, both states of mind that are unstable and undesirable, and likely to give rise to unpredictable behaviour that may be extreme, and will definitely be dangerous to both horse and human.

Given Star's background, I already know that there is an existing negative emotional association with being handled, and a strong motivation to avoid it. If this factor is not taken into account there will be problems. Star's state of mind is insufficiently sound for her to cope.

If I employ this 'quick fix' of just getting on with it, and making her accept handling when she is not emotionally ready, I will undermine all of the work I have invested in building her trust of me. She will not understand if I give signals which ask her to trust me, but then ask her to do something that makes her scared.

There are many instances of existing training methods and techniques where this happens. For example, when walking with our horse we want him to not crowd us; other times we ask that he come close to us: this causes confusuion and uncertainty about when he should come to us, and when to keep his distance? If we then reinforce our request that he stay away with waving arms that startle and alarm him, is it any wonder that he is reluctant to engage with us?

Using such a method with Star would only reinforce her view that being handled is scary and unsafe, and that she is right to be afraid. She will also be unable to learn when in this heightened state, so there is little point in trying to teach her

Consistency is key to gaining trust. (Courtesy Andy Francis)

anything, as it simply won't work. Even if she should be capable of containing and managing her emotions, the same issues remain: this is a scary thing, and she does not like it. Earlier, I talked about stress, and the effects it has on the body and mind, which also applies here. If episodes like this occur too often, we will have a horse who is stressed more often than not, with all the associated problems that this brings.

Another problem will be avoidance: we all try to avoid doing things that we don't like doing, and a horse is no different in this respect. Catching sight of me approaching her with the headcollar, Star may simply avoid me so that I am unable to put it on her, refusing to walk to the tie-up location, perhaps, or stop coming in from the field. When working behaviourally, we must take motivation, emotion, and reinforcement into consideration in order to achieve our goals.

THREE STEP STRATEGY

This is how I am going to deal with Star's current aversion to handling, using a strategy which involves three behavioural techniques –

* Make everything that happens (handling, touching, grooming, checking legs, etc) part of the general routine, but not every time or at a set time. In this way, whatever it is becomes normal, and part of the day. Star does not learn to anticipate this as it's not a regular occurrence, so she does not become anxious about it, making it less of an issue.
* Always do the things she dislikes after something she does like. If I stroke her when I'm giving her some hay, her attention is focused on the food rather than the touch, ensuring her mood is one of contentment rather than anxiety: what seems a big deal

A tale of two horses

when it is anticipated loses its impact when she is not worrying about it.

- Never reach her tolerance threshold. If I always stop doing something that Star is anxious/worried about before she finds it too much to bear, the bad associations and connotations will be replaced by less traumatic feelings.

The principle behind this strategy is to work sub-threshold, at a level which does not trigger any negative responses, which means I have spent time simply standing next to Star, as touching her triggers an adverse reaction. Once she becomes accustomed to me being around her, I can stand closer, then progress to a touch, which, to start with, lasts only about a second. Progression goes at Star's pace, because if she does not feel anxious or scared by what I am doing, existing behaviours and emotions attached to this will not be reinforced, allowing her to change her perception of what's happening, and form positive associated emotions and behaviours.

All three steps in the programme are adjusted as necessary, or I run the risk of making Star more reactive, or transferring her anxiety to the things she does like. After doing this for a while, Star is now able to stand still whilst I stroke or groom her, though is still very sure that she does not want me to pick up her feet, and attempts to do this result in her walking away.

She will stand when Clive, the barefoot trimmer, comes to trim her hooves, but is not at all relaxed or happy. This is not something that I want to promote, by ignoring it and simply hoping she gets used to it, as it again means that negative emotions and associations are being reinforced. Fundamentally, this will have an impact if she injures herself and pain is involved, with the very likely result that, as she merely tolerated this before such an incident, she will not let me anywhere near her feet afterward. So now I need to change her perception about having her feet picked up.

Having achieved calmness at being touched, it is a simple case of applying the same three-rule

Building a bond based on trust and mutual respect. (Courtesy Andy Francis)

strategy to teach Star that there is nothing to worry about with having her feet done. I start off by gently running my hand down her leg, a little at a time. I never try to do more each time, and sometimes don't even go near her legs, so that she remains calm, and has no need to feel uneasy when being touched.

Once I have progressed down her legs, I try to lift a foot a little, then put it straight back down. Again, I will not do this every time, and may lift a different foot. I tell her she's a clever girl and keep everything matter of fact. If I place too much importance on this she is going to notice and react. Trying to achieve a specific target by a certain time will apply unnecessary pressure: we will get there when we get there.

Horses, dogs and cats all have the ability to 'smell a rat,' and know when something is going on. We know that what we are trying to achieve is important, building anticipation and expectation; wondering whether or not our animal will comply. We usually get a bit stressed, too, and this affects our body language and tone of voice. For example, have you ever witnessed an owner trying to call their dog to them, whilst the animal studiously ignores their commands, or even takes off in the opposite direction? Becoming more and more stressed (and even a little angry), the owner resorts to shouting at the dog to 'Come!' in a tone of voice, and displaying body language, that is not at all inviting. It's no wonder that the dog decides against going anywhere near them! Remembering how they normally get their animal to come, and using a voice command along with a toy or titbit of food as an incentive as usual, would have the desired effect in no time. Unfortunately, we can behave differently when doing something we consider important, and this is very, very obvious to our animals.

When teaching recall, a useful training strategy is to turn around and walk away from your dog if he is not responding. Generally, he will wonder where you're going and follow you, thus achieving your objective (although only the basics, this is a good foundation on which to build). Of course, in a situation where safety is an issue, you do what you

Calling your dog but he just stands there? Walk away and it's likely he'll follow you.

must to resolve the situation, but if you don't make a big deal of something, neither will your dog, cat or horse.

It's always beneficial to play to species-specific behaviour. Horses, for example, are naturally inquisitive, so all I have to do to get them to take notice is turn around and ignore them. Lo and behold, they're soon nosing around, investigating what's going on.

STEADY PROGRESSION = LASTING RESULTS

Star really is a star, who has gone from being unable to stand still if she thinks I'm going near her legs, to calmly standing, eating hay whilst I pick up all four feet, one after the other. She's calm, relaxed, and does not feel the need to walk away afterwards,

A tale of two horses

Horses are inquisitive, and will often try to become involved if they feel ignored!

sounds very sweet, and obviously enjoyable for him. Up until now, he had been been putting his nose in the bucket, unable to wait for the food to be tipped out, but is now waiting for me to do this (although he can't do so for long, and the bucket gets a little push with his nose if I'm too slow!).

There is still competition between the horses, but the dynamic has changed from Charlie being in charge (he got to the food first, and Star was told to go away if she came too close), to Star taking charge, with Charlie deferring to her.

Star is not happy for Charlie to be near when they are in the field with me. If I'm with Charlie, and Star comes over to us I have to move away, and if I am near Star and Charlie comes over, again, I have to move away. If I remain when Charlie and Star are close to each other, Star will find this too difficult, and try and kick Charlie.

Aside from the competition over resources such as food and me, the relationship between the two of them is growing stronger. Charlie is very affectionate with Star, giving her lots of gentle snuggling and nibbling, which, surprisingly, Star is now quite receptive to, and they've spent quite a lot of time together. Ah, spoke too soon: Star has come into season and is kicking at Charlie if he comes anywhere near her. She is highly strung, excitable, and intolerant!

A DIFFERENT PERSPECTIVE

Despite Star being difficult now she is in season, a lot of positive progress has been made. But it's always beneficial to have a different perspective, and a good way of assessing how you are actually progressing is observation by someone who does not see the horses on a frequent basis, who will notice the changes that those of us who are with them often don't.

Graham is our lovely pest control man, who also has his own horses. He visits on a regular basis, but does not always have the time to say hello to Charlie and Star. At the end of the previous year we realised that our efforts to prevent the local rat population from making our farm its permanent

either. This is another success and, importantly, I'm developing really strong behavioural foundations to build on, increasing my trustworthiness with behaviour that is reassuringly consistent.

Things are progressing well. It's now April and I feel that Charlie and Star have greater trust in me, being less wary, and actively seeking attention from me. They are calmer, too, though we still have a long way to go here.

Charlie has started making little nickering noises when he receives his Speedi-Beet®, which residence were not really working. I'm not sure what alerted us to this: the fact that the dogs had a small audience whilst they ate their meals every day, maybe, or it could have been the sight of baby rats following their elders about, clearly learning the ropes when it came to finding food. It could have been seeing them sunning themselves in the greenhouse, or even when they appeared to gaze longingly through the lounge window of an evening when we sat down to watch the television. Whatever the reason, at some point we decided we needed Graham's help.

His initial visit, which involved a good amount of head shaking and exclamations about the state of things, happened to be on the same day that Charlie and Star arrived.

Fortunately, Graham's investigations revealed that the rats had made their home in a different part of the farm to where the horses were to be kept, because that area clearly afforded them good sunbathing opportunities and a regular supply of healthy snacks (chicken feed).

So, Graham saw the horses on day one, and was also instantly appointed Chief Rat Catcher. During a routine visit in the spring to check that the rats had not returned after their eviction, he went along and visited the horses, too. His opinion was that Charlie and Star were very different animals to when they first arrived: holding themselves more confidently, and apparently much happier and content. It was really nice, he said, that, not having seen them for a while, what a big difference there was. A good indication that things were progressing well.

Busy time on the farm

It's not, of course, just about horses on the farm. It's lambing time for us – very late, compared to most – but we are not a commercial farm, and do not have to adhere to the rather inconvenient practice of having lambs being born in the winter so that they are ready for the shops in spring (for us, 'spring lamb' refers to when they are born, not when they are eaten). I'm sure I don't need to point out

how much more work, time and money is involved in housing and feeding ewes and lambs over the winter, but we don't get involved in this as we lamb in spring, when the weather is warm enough for babies to be outside, and there is plenty of grass for their mums to eat. The pregnant ladies are looking like they've swallowed buses sideways, and are clearly ready to have their babies. Hebrideans are very good at birthing without problems, so the process should be nice and easy again this year.

My animal care methodology is the same for every species. For example, if I have my dog hat on the training is reward-based; I use only positive-reinforcement, and the same applies to how I train my horses. It is important that every animal in my care receives the same standard of welfare, and is trained using the same methods. Apart from the fact

All of our animals are handled with the same positive methods, to bring out the best of their abilities and personality.

A tale of two horses

that every animal has the right to not suffer abuse or mistreatment, all mammals learn in the same way; I already know the most efficient and effective way of doing things so why would my methods vary?

Regarding keeping and raising livestock for food, many different views exist, and most people will not wish to know about the animals that ultimately end up on their table. We see both sides to this situation, as we both raise animals and eat meat, and firmly believe that any living animal has the right to the highest level of welfare, which also includes emotional welfare. I cannot withhold affection and care from the food animals on our farm for this very reason.

William, the ram, has been brought up in the same way as have my dogs and cats, and Charlie and Star. William is a lovely ram: well-balanced and content; happy to be handled, comes when called, and is safe to be around in the field. He's happy enough on his own, or when he's in the company of his youngsters or his ladies. We don't spend hours running around trying to catch him if he needs medication, and he'll stand quietly for the vet on the odd occasion he needs to be seen by him.

Perhaps this is not the usual perception of a ram, but if you work in harmony with animals you can achieve pretty much anything. However, if your mindset comprises expectations formed by species or breed reputation, and you base your training ideals on these, you may create a tricky situation that could easily have been avoided. This is not to say, of course, that all animals are capable of achieving great things, or that they will respond in the same way (there'd certainly be no need for animal behaviourists if this was the case ...).

Larry is William's son. Should it follow that his temperament will be similar to that of his dad? No: genetics are never that simple, and hereditary characteristics do not always present as one might expect. Larry has had the same learning experiences as William, but has not developed in the same way. Whereas William engages his thinking brain, Larry's viewpoint is more strongly influenced by the emotional part of the brain; he is quicker to respond in an instinctive way, and so is less predictable than William. We don't go into Larry's field in the same way as we do William's, for example, and everything we do with Larry takes into account his personality, to allow him to achieve his best. In this way, we avoid situations where things can go wrong.

So whatever I am faced with, the same principles and methods are applied, adjusted to suit each animal's personality. This is the beauty of all life: the pleasure of getting to know and understand each individual animal.

ASSOCIATIONS AND DIRECTIONAL CUES

Charlie and Star are beginning to understand us more, too. I talk to them all the time, repeating the same phrases when doing things so that they soon start to pick up on the association. This approach is a big part of how I teach dogs. It's important to teach specific behaviours such as sit, down, etc, but what really makes the difference between a brilliantly-trained dog and one who is always getting into trouble is all the stuff in-between these behaviours, which I call lifestyle skills. For example, having these skills means that Indie can distinguish between the barn, the shed and the garage. If I ask him where his dad is he first looks around, then back to me if he can't see him. I then tell him which building Matt is in, and off he goes to find him.

If you apply this strategy to everything you do with your dog, he will learn, 'this way,' 'that way,' 'up the hill,' 'to the pond,' etc, very quickly and easily, which means I have much more control when my dog is off-lead, as he understands these words and phrases, and knows what to do when I say them. To me, conversation is education.

It also means that an animal is more fulfilled if he has things to do to stimulate his mind, and as he is choosing to do these things himself, rather than being coerced, his self-confidence and sense of security are increased, minimising the potential for anxiety. And by applying the same learning principles to my horses, I can achieve the equivalent level of understanding and response that I have with Indie.

I've been told that horses don't generally

respond to their names, so trying for anything more than this is pointless. However, this is not the case at all. Not only do Charlie and Star know their names, they are learning phrases such as 'this side,' and 'other side;' 'excuse me,' 'I'm behind you,' and 'breakfast.'

Thinking about species specifics, when teaching we should adjust for differences in breed, also. Take dogs: generally, Collies are very quick to respond, their minds ready and waiting for something to engage them. On the other hand, with Indie, a Great Dane, the message has to get from his brain to his very long limbs, which takes time! Clearly, this statement is not based in science, as the speed at which messages are sent and received along neural pathways is not determined by animal size. But the fact remains, terriers and Collies tend to be super-quick at all they do, and larger, slower breeds take a little longer to perform the behaviour. Whippets are slow to sit – well, they've got bony bums! As pups, terriers tend not to learn a relaxed sit with their bum firmly on the ground because they usually have them up in the air ready to dive down rabbit holes: not at all conducive to sitting on the floor in a relaxed way. A Staffie's body shape often means he prefers not to lie down completely, so he will adopt a half-down position, or fully down with legs to one side.

Bearing in mind these differences, is it reasonable to expect exactly the same response from each different dog? No, and if I did I would have a fair few unsuccessful training sessions, not to mention disgruntled clients. The same concept applies to our horses: different breeds respond in different timescales, and in different ways.

Once I have Charlie's and Star's attention, and they are moving, they're not really slow, although, initially, their reaction is somewhat delayed. When this happens, Matt looks at me as if to say "Well, they did that then" (although they clearly did not), to which I usually respond "Give them chance, they're quite big, you know, and it takes time!"

A lack of response may be due to the fact that they are not focused on me as much as I would like, and their brains need time to take in and

comprehend what I have said. Also, asked-for new behaviours require more time to compute and carry out. They may be able to process what I've asked for and respond appropriately, or lose focus and think about something else. The same is true in dog class. I often tell owners not to be so quick to decide that their dog has not listened to their instruction: waiting a little longer gives their dog time to understand and then perform the behaviour asked for. As the behaviour becomes more familiar, we can then train for a quicker response, if this is what's required.

GET THE ATTENTION; GET THE BEHAVIOUR
Another thing to overcome in horses is their ability to 'zone out,' which I suspect that every horse owner has witnessed. There are two instances when Charlie and Star do this: standing in the pouring rain, apparently completely oblivious to the rain, and the notion that, perhaps, they should seek shelter, and when they are grazing, and seem completely deaf to my shouts for them to come in.

If you have had the privilege to be around different horse breeds, you may have noticed that some are quite good at getting out of bad weather and some don't seem to have a clue. This comes down to instinct and breed origins, unless they have been taught this behaviour. Before domestication, horses were responsible for their own well-being and survival, of course, and those who lived in harsh climates wouldn't have survived for long if they stood out in the most exposed spots. Those breeds indigenous to more temperate climates would not have had this conditioning, so are less likely to seek shelter from inclement weather.

'Zoning out' when grazing is an entirely different matter, and it's often the case that the horses are so engrossed in what they are doing, they simply don't register anything else. A good analogy is a dog scenting. When you let your dog off his lead in the park, I bet the first thing he does is run around sniffing everything. There's little point trying to get his attention whilst he's doing this, as his brain is so taken up with the stimuli, he simply does not hear you. The same goes for horses: they are usually very

Charlie can listen and respond to me once I have his attention.

Get the attention, get the behaviour.
(Courtesy Andy Francis)

Dogs love to run about, scenting everything in sight.

Newborn lambs – aren't they sweet?

serious about the activity of eating after sunrise and before dusk – breakfast and supper – particularly important times of the day for grazing, and they go about this with more enthusiasm than at other times. Their entire focus is on this, and, although obviously aware of their surroundings, their ears are tuned to pick up only those noises that represent a threat or should not be there, so unless you make a noise that is out of the ordinary, your voice may be regarded as background noise. The key to working through this is to first get their attention (being close enough for them to notice you, or making an unusual sound so that they look up), and then you can ask for the behaviour.

Now back to those lambs that were about to be born! We have nine so far – so sweet; little black bundles of loveliness! They are born with their horns already starting to show, so it's usually quite easy to see which are the boys as they have more of a stump than the girls. Mums are doing fine and breathing a sigh of relief to be a normal size again, I think!

Life on the farm is really quite rewarding when you are able to work in harmony with nature, and have the time to appreciate it.

Of course, it is even better now that I have Charlie and Star, too!

Chapter 7

Stable routine

It's now May, and we've settled into a nice routine over recent months.

The last of the lambs have been born, and we have fifteen of them leaping and skipping about the place. All the mums are doing well, and seem very pleased with themselves. We haven't had to help anyone, and haven't actually seen many of the lambs being born: the ewes really prefer to be left to get on with it themselves, so will cross their legs and wait for you to leave them in peace to do so!

Rosie, one of the ewes, has once again taken on nanny duties, and is often found with the lambs whilst the other mums are grazing. She's happy to feed anyone who asks, and her milk bar is rather well stocked, as you might imagine!

It has been incredibly wet, so the summer field remains empty until the grass has grown sufficiently for a first cut, and before the horses move in. As they are still in the winter field (where there is not that much grass), the morning routine is hay and Speedi-Beet® for breakfast, then mucking out. The pigs and chickens also need breakfast, and cuddles (well, the pigs: they like nothing more than a nice back rub, after which they give themselves a good shake, flinging mud all over me. I swear they are laughing! Pigs do have a cheeky sense of humour). The chickens look at me in alarm if it seems I'm going to pick them up: my presence is obviously not a reassuring one as Matt doesn't get the same reaction, and a couple of our cockerels even quite like being picked up by him, it seems.

And speaking of routine, we have one with Indie when the weather is bad. Everyone should exercise to stay healthy, and our animals are no different, but trying to get two reluctant dogs to go out in the pouring rain is not so easy: delicately poking their noses outside the door and spying the rain, they quickly back up and retreat to their beds the moment a raindrop falls on them! Since moving to North Devon, however, we have discovered that it rains here most of the time, so we began changing Indie's and Coco's perception of rain. By playing with their toys outside, it wasn't long before they were more interested in playing than being bothered about the rain. Great: a result already. Ahh, not so fast: a quick play, then they both turned round and went back inside. Over the next few days I made it really interesting for them to be outside, whether or not it was raining, and soon enough they didn't even notice the rain, happily coming out for a walk or play, whatever the weather. It's a different matter with Matt, however, who is still very reluctant to go out when it's raining hard, moaning and groaning about getting wet. Perhaps I'll take a beer with me – he's bound to follow that!

What started as a joke – saying we must do our daily exercise as we walked – was picked up on by the dogs, who associated the phrase with going for a walk around the field. Once I realised this, I began saying it before we went out, and, sure enough, there the two of them would be, standing outside the door with waggy tails, waiting for us to hurry up and begin the walk! Since that time, Coco our rescue German Shepherd cross, has passed away, and Indie is now considered elderly for his breed, and suffers from some joint stiffness, but the daily exercise continues, even if he's not as keen some days.

Anyway, on this particular day we'd had torrential rain since breakfast, and now, past lunchtime, Indie still hadn't done anything other than take a quick wander around the garden, so Matt and I decided to see if he could manage at least one walk. We set off, telling Indie that we were going to do our daily exercise, and, surprisingly, he came with us, accompanied by lots of praise and encouragement from us. Charlie and Star looked at us from the doorway of the barn, and I could imagine them thinking: "They've got him out, then, they must be mad! Hope they don't try to make us walk round the field in this." At this point I think Indie's enthusiasm ran out, because as we got to the field and I said, as usual, "Come on then, daily exercise," he took off at full pelt, and by the time we had gone a third of the way into the field, he was at the other end. Expecting him to stay there and wait for us, we were astonished to see him run around the entire perimeter of the field, and straight back out through the gate! Once we'd stopped laughing, we made our soggy way back to find Indie settled in his bed, daily exercise done, to the letter, all the way around the field!

After that it was back to work, and the usual daily check on the animals.

Strawberry: happy after recovering from a twisted ankle.

DEVELOPING TRUST AND AWARENESS

I walked down the lane this particular morning to discover that Strawberry, the cow, was limping quite badly. She must have been in some considerable pain, too, as she didn't come over when I put down the hay. Oh dear, it looked like she had a rather large abscess on her leg, a little way above her hoof. Not knowing what to do about this, I called the vet.

David arrived a while later, along with a newly-qualified vet who was working with him. David is well aware of our approach with the animals, and happy to go along with doing things in such a way that causes them the least amount of upset. The

young vet beside him, however, had no idea what he was letting himself in for …

"Where is Strawberry?" asked David. "In the end field," I tell him as we walk down the lane. The ground is really, really soggy from all the rain we've been having, and as the cows' feet sink much further into the mire than horses, the areas they use a lot are just a pool of sticky mud.

"So," I say, "we can either climb over the gate – although the entrance is churned mud up to our calves – or we can go over the bank and over the fence." David laughs, as the trailing vet looks horrified; thinking, I'm sure, that he didn't sign up for this, and why was the cow not tied up in a barn? "We'll go over the bank, then," David declares. An excellent choice! So the three of us scramble up the bank, over the other side, through the ditch and over the fence into the field. Vet number two looks on rather dubiously and asks: "Will she just stand there?" "Oh, yes," I reply, with complete confidence, "she can't walk." "Usually, they are tied up, he observes. "She doesn't need tying up, she's quite calm," I assert.

Cows can be as placid as you like with people they know, but are very wary with people they don't, so the vet had a point. But I had a secret weapon – a bucket of her favourite biscuits. I offer Strawberry the bucket and she has a taste, then looks at the vets and limps a couple of steps. Ruby is happily munching hers on the other side of the field so doesn't get in the way. We leave Strawberry for a minute to settle and get started on her biscuits. She is fine, so I pick up the affected leg, exactly as I do with the horses, to check there's nothing in her hoof. David is easily able to look at her leg, as she is very happy eating, and not taking any notice of us. His diagnosis is that the lump is not an abscess but a calcium deposit, and nothing to worry about. As she may also have twisted her foot, David prescribes painkillers, and I am to monitor her condition.

As we walk back across the field, David comments on how good Strawberry has been: usually when he has to treat a cow in a field it involves his chasing around, trying to catch the animal, so this was a first for him!

It turns out that Strawberry has indeed twisted her foot, and a few days later she is back to normal and running about as usual.

I believe that Strawberry was content to stand and be treated by David because there were enough familiar and reliable pointers to reassure her that the situation was fairly normal, and enable her to remain calm and not panic. What I mean by this is that animals will rely on those they know and are familiar with for comfort, friendship and safety, because they have developed an association with those around them. They may only know them in the sense that a given situation is normal and as it should be: the sheep they are used to seeing in the next field are always there, for example, or, they may have developed more of a relationship with another horse who has been contained in the same field as them.

When learning something new – be this a movement, understanding of a word, becoming used to the environment, or developing relationships – the same process happens, as the brain gets to know the new thing in context with everything else. When teaching a horse a new movement, initially, these will be associated not only with the cue given for it, but also where the teaching is occurring, and what is going on around, along with the emotional state they are in at the time: quite a few factors are involved. It may also be the case that a horse will work better and more productively in the morning, as this is what he is familiar with, and if training is done at a different time, he may not be as confident and relaxed, and the training will not go as well. To progress this situation, it is necessary to teach him that he can perform the same movement out of context, which, in this case, is a different time of the day. He is then able to understand that he can do the same thing when in a slightly different situation. From here, progress to asking for the movement in plenty of different situations, so that he effectively learns the movement in isolation, without any associations.

A behaviour is not properly known until it is possible to separate it from those associations that are created as the behaviour is learnt, and perform it regardless of location and situation. Emotions work in the same way: the brain will attach associations to them, so if your horse was badly scared by a particular event, place or situation, a link with that emotion is established, and the fact that this may have been a one-off – a car backfired, say – is immaterial, and the horse may absolutely refuse to go near the place where this occurred.

Thinking of our own behaviour, when out of our comfort zone, we may try and find something familiar to reassure ourselves that all is well – turning round and going home, for example! Horses may seek out a familiar horse with whom they have a relationship, may move towards their owner, or stand in a part of the field that has positive and safe associations.

These reactions are all part of the learning process, demonstrating an ability to try and cope with an unfamiliar situation or event by doing or seeking something familiar. Sometimes, however, this is not coping at all, but is actually opting out and choosing to avoid rather than deal with a situation, which can make things difficult for us as owners and trainers when we need our horse to be able to deal with different or worrying situations. It's no good if our horse's default strategy is to run home as fast as possible every time he sees a car, for example, or he refuses to be caught whenever he sees the horsebox.

So what can we do about this?

DESENSITISATION AND COUNTER-CONDITIONING

Being able to cope and adapt to whatever the situation demands, and not default to a 'safe' position is much more difficult to do, and a further progression of the learning process. The basics are already in place if we have taught our horse to do things in different places, as we have changed the context of when and where things can be done. The next step is to help him develop a coping strategy for when he is in situations that he feels worried about, which will give him the ability to come up with an alternative response to that he would normally have, as well as take the focus off the problem situation.

Simply expecting him to get used to the situation if he experiences it often enough is not effective – or kind. I am absolutely terrified of spiders, to the extent that they have to be removed from a room if I am in it: I simply cannot stay in that room if a spider is there, and I can tell you I see very many of the creepy things on the farm. I opened the front door to a caller the other day, and immediately closed it again, shouting "ARRGGHHH!" at the sight of hundreds (maybe a slight exaggeration) of spiders on the outside of the door. The poor caller was still looking confused by the time I'd gone out the back door (no spiders there) and walked round

to the front. The point is, of course, that although I have been in this world for 40 years and seen many thousands of spiders, my perception of them has not changed: they still terrify me. What has changed, however, is my reaction to them: a much less extreme version of what it used to be, and I don't go into an all-out panic any more (though I still cannot actually deal with them). This is what desensitisation is: being around something long enough until you eventually get used – desensitised – to it. An okay strategy, in theory, but I don't really want to wait that long for my horses to get used to something, or put them through the trauma every time.

And this approach can also actually make a horse more, rather than less, sensitive to the problem if carried out the wrong way. Desensitisation has very limited effect when dealing with negative and fearful emotions, as it relies on a gradual decrease in the strength of the emotional and physical response to the scary object or situation. In order to be an effective method, it needs to be used in conjunction with a strategy of counter-conditioning (widely used by positive-method trainers), which takes the focus off the problem and provides an alternative, thus changing the perception around the object or situation, whilst the horse becomes used to it. It is a very effective technique when used properly, and an essential tool when working with many issues.

The end result of using desensitisation on its own or as a combination strategy may appear be the same on the surface, but not in the horse's mind. If decreased sensitivity has been achieved by only working on the desensitisation aspect, only a tolerance of the situation may have occurred, and just one negative experience could send sensitivity rocketing. You may also find that the tolerance level will gradually reduce, making the animal more reactive, in which case, the remedy often used is to give a reward of some sort in order to reassure the horse or dog, and prevent a further decrease in tolerance.

Unfortunately, this only causes conflict. The scary thing prompts a desire to get away from

A tale of two horses

it (aversion behaviour), whilst, in order to receive the reward, the animal must overcome this instinct (creating conflict).

This way of working provides too much room for things to go wrong. The potential for the horse to associate the reward (and possibly his owner) with the actual problem is high, with the result that he not only views the situation we are trying to desensitise him to as worrying, but also won't go near the reward, and becomes wary of us, too: an association he may apply to other contexts. Working with owners, sometimes matters have deteriorated to the extent that a horse is generally wary, and increasingly reluctant to do anything his owner wants him to. The owner compensates for this by trying harder to coerce him, which only reinforces the horse's view that he should remain wary!

Attempting to decrease sensitivity and reactivity should be attempted in conjunction with counter-conditioning: ie distract and refocus, teaching our horse a range of appropriate strategies, and giving him the means to cope and know what to do in situations that are not familiar. By doing this we teach him to be confident around new objects and situations, and, more importantly, confident in himself, so that he is sure of his own ability to cope.

Having already taught our horse lots of different movements and things he can do, and in different places, the next step is to apply these movements and actions to the problem we need to resolve. For example, if our horse can't cope with cars, begin working at a distance from a car, sufficiently far enough away from it that he is not anxious, but close enough so that he can see it. This is the desensitisation part, and is known as working at sub-threshold. Ask the horse to perform some movements that are easy and enjoyable for him to do, to distract him from the car and refocus his attention. This is the counter-conditioning part.

At this stage the objective is for our horse to maintain a positive emotional state, and for him to take no notice of the car. Once achieved, we get a little closer to the car and repeat the process. It is essential to work at each stage long enough for our

horse to be completely comfortable and unworried by the car before progressing. If he shows any signs of not coping and the beginnings of anxiety, move further away again immediately. The same approach can be used if our horse runs in the opposite direction the moment he sees the horsebox or trailer. It doesn't take long, just a few days' work, to teach him that he does not need to worry about the scary thing, and that he can do other things and refocus his mind on those rather than the problem. Of course, the more severe the problem, the longer it will take to resolve. Patience is the key word here – attempt to rush it and we will probably make matters worse.

In the case of a car-shy horse, we want to get to the point where our horse can focus on us, and do other things, whilst taking no notice of the car, but in the case of the horsebox, of course, we do need him to take notice of it, as he has to get in it. Once we are able to work with him in close proximity to the box without him displaying any signs of anxiety or stress, we can then work with his natural inquisitiveness. If he's not afraid of the horsebox and we leave it open, he may decide to take a closer look of his own volition. Horses always like to help, so if working about and around the box, not asking anything of him, we may well find that he will follow us about, 'helping.' Dropping some hay on the ramp as we work, it may be that he will stand with his forelegs on the ramp, whilst he takes advantage of our carelessness. We want him to think it was all his idea, and we're not trying to get him to do anything (if he thinks he is being enticed he's likely to back off). Reward the behaviour sought, and work towards him walking into the trailer willingly, of his own accord.

This type of work will increase his self-confidence, as well as many other aspects of equine behaviour. That's the great thing about working in this way: everything is linked, so improvements in other areas often result, without needing to work directly on them.

This is the reason why David, our vet, could examine Strawberry's bad leg whilst she was loose in the field. She has enough self-confidence not to spook and run away (although it would have been more of a hobble than a run!), and the familiarity of her favourite biscuits and me reassured her, confirming her perception that all was okay.

I'm not as far down this road, yet, with Charlie and Star, but I'm getting there. Star is less reactive if Charlie is not in her direct line of sight, which shows her self-confidence and coping strategies are beginning to emerge.

Changing perceptions – a challenge
The horses tend to wander, and have a doze around noon most days. They're usually quite relaxed around this time, so I've been spending more time bonding with them, and ignoring the jobs I should be doing. It's very important to develop our relationship, and they are just so lovely I simply can't keep away. I am doing something useful, too: grooming them, and

being around them helps to build our relationship ... as I tell Matt when he comes in from work and asks what I've been doing all day ...

At these times, Indie likes to lie out in the grass (if it stops raining long enough), or stretch out on the hay in the barn whilst I'm busy with the horses. He really is a perfect dog, and I've always ensured he is included in my interaction with Charlie and Star.

And now for something completely different ...
But now I really do have to get on, and so, reluctantly, I head back indoors for something completely different – an art exhibition to finish organising and host, and I didn't realise just how much work goes into something like this. I teach two art classes a week and, since the previous autumn, we have been working towards painting enough

Indie relaxes whilst I spend time with Charlie and Star.

pieces to fill the large town hall. I teach adults, some of whom have painted before, and some of whom are novices. All have their own style and preferred subject matter, so there's a huge variety in the work for display. We're about there: the last few pieces are being finished and the count is 124 paintings. Not bad for a small group of fifteen artists.

I know I couldn't do this on my own, there really is so much to do, so we have an 'easel team.' All of our pieces are mounted, though not framed, so we can't hang them from the walls, and, even if we could, I don't think we'd fit all of them on. So we've decided on a table layout for the hall, with walkways and aisles to make it interesting, and make the best use of the space. The only problem with this is that there is nothing to stand the paintings up against, as the tables are not along the walls. Our solution to this was to make easels to put them all on, which was quite a big job, but they look really professional and display the paintings well.

Our art group also has a layout and catalogue team, a set-up team, a take-down team, a catering team, and allocated people for the day rota, evening rota, and to serve food and drink (we've decided that a good way to attract people is to offer free tea and cake!).

We also have someone who is a whizz on painting and drawing software on the computer, so he's in charge of producing all the adverts, the catalogue, artist bios, prints, and cards of original works. This is the biggest job of all, as, along with producing all of the advertising, he has to scan each piece of artwork and prepare it to print on cards, and as different-sized prints. It has been such a lot of work organising and checking everything is in place, but it should be worth it, and everyone is really excited about showing their work for the first time. We've decided on a public viewing during the day, and a private viewing in the evening for family and friends. With everything done, all we have to do now is wait for the date to arrive.

Evenings at home still begin with my usual "My horses …" to which Matt is still amenable (although he really must be bored after several

months of this). He lets me chatter on, bless him, up to the point when he really has heard enough horse talk, and will exclaim "Enough!" The days are lovely and long, so we have several walks before it gets dark. Indie loves being out, and it's good exercise for us, plus I get to see my horses more, too!

EMOTIONAL STATES

Star has discovered that running holds no fear. Previously, when she ran, she would automatically shift up into that extra gear that racehorses have, her head down, and galloping very fast in a straight line, after which she always became subdued: quiet; running because she needed to, rather than because she wanted to. There never seemed to be any pleasure in it for her, it was as if she just had to get through it. Charlie would run with her, but she would take no notice of him, almost as if she was saying that running was a serious business, and to stop messing about! Charlie would really have fun, and carry on with a canter or a trot, shaking his head and neighing. Star simply stood when she stopped, not looking in the least bit happy or content.

However, having realised that she can run and nothing bad happens, she gallops, prances, kicks out her back legs, and thoroughly enjoys herself. She still goes from standstill to a full gallop, which is exceedingly impressive, but her body shape and body language are very different; now it's for the sheer pleasure that she runs, playing and enjoying herself rather than doing a job. It's so good to see.

Star does, however, still experience negative associations with other emotions.

For the first time since the horses had arrived, I went away for the weekend, leaving Matt in charge, and everything went well, as expected. When I came back I was desperate to see Charlie and Star. Would they take any notice of me? Would they be happy that I had returned, or was I just someone to feed them? Having already fallen in love with them, I was desperate for them to love me back!

To my delight, Charlie greeted me with the whinny he reserves for the very best thing in his life: his breakfast bucket of Speedi-Beet®. He doesn't make this sound at any other time – it's obviously an expression of how happy he is – and on this occasion, it was me who prompted a demonstration of it! He gave me a lovely rub with his head and nuzzle. Yippee, he *does* love me!

Star, however, behaved in a very different way. She did what she used to do when she couldn't cope: she walked away. I was quite surprised at this, expecting, if not a greeting, then for her to ignore me and carry on eating, but, no, she reverted to her previous default behaviour.

Maybe the change in routine had been stressful for her, and my return caused her to feel relief? Perhaps she did feel happy to see me, but it was all a bit too much? Whatever the emotion she was experiencing, she clearly could not cope with it. It didn't take long before she was fine, again, thank goodness, but this incident clearly demonstrated that we were still in the early stages.

The lambs are now five to six weeks old and run around like little race cars. Charlie and Star look on bemused, as if to say "Good grief, what on earth are they doing now?" The lambs get everywhere; there really is no containing them. They've been up and down my A frame (agility equipment) at full speed, and much quicker than the dogs I teach. Maybe I should do agility with lambs instead? They seem to have no fear – or brakes!

Charlie has changed tremendously. He holds himself well and is more confident. He looks at me, maintains eye contact, talks, and instigates interaction, trusting me enough to let me see his personality. He is quite tactile, and is usually close by when I'm out with the two of them, happy to mooch about near me, and not wander off as much as he did. He's lost the wariness he had, and is more relaxed and happy to stay around. He interacts with me, and has started to ask for affection when I feed him instead of saying "Go away, I'm eating."

A word of warning here, though. Charlie is staying close when I'm about, and asking for affection for more than the obvious reason. Yes, he likes seeing what I'm doing and getting involved (horses are naturally inquisitive, and love to help – or

This little chap must be the cutest lamb ever.

hinder, as the case may be!), but the other emotion at play here is insecurity. This way of being around me is new, which tells me that, along with all the positive, nice emotions Charlie is feeling, he's also a little unsure and insecure. This is usual for anyone, person or animal, when in a new situation that is not yet established and familiar, or when they are being brave and doing something extra in an already

A tale of two horses

3-5-week-old lambs.

familiar situation. Charlie is comfortable and familiar enough to open up and interact, but it is still a little worrying for him at this early stage.

At this point Charlie is susceptible to developing a dependency on things he finds reassuring, and this is not necessarily a good thing. As he becomes more comfortable with the situation he can progress in one of two ways: he develops his own sense of self-confidence and becomes more sure of his abilities, and therefore more able to rely on himself, and not panic when in unknown situations, or cope with his feelings of insecurity by using something as an emotional crutch, rather than develop his self-confidence. It is this emotional crutch that I have to watch out for, and it is me – and not Charlie – who has to be monitored: I'll explain why.

When Charlie is being brave, it's very easy for me to reassure, support and encourage him with love and care, feeling really happy that he is getting braver, and doing all I can to help him. But if I am too supportive I will not help him to become braver, but rather make him dependent on me for the means by which he can be brave. As we can all appreciate, it's much easier to rely on someone else for support than do something on your own (as I would do sometimes, with Matt), so encouraging Charlie to develop a dependency on me as an emotional crutch is not helping him at all; quite the reverse. It's

no good if Charlie can't do things without me: what happens when I am not here, and Matt has to attend to him?

It's good to be able to count on someone to support you, but not at the cost of being unable to develop self-confidence and cope on your own. Once in this cycle of dependency it's hard to get out of it, and the longer it goes on the more difficult it is to learn to rely on ourself. What I need to develop in this situation is Charlie's self-reliance, with me there in the background to assist when necessary, but not to do things for him. I must encourage Charlie to continue being brave and do things for himself, and work out what action to take if he does get worried, without giving him the opportunity to develop emotional dependency on me.

Correct perceptions

Star has progressed well, too; she has become more confident in herself, and no longer sticks like glue to Charlie, happy to wander away from him rather than stay very close. She has also learnt how to reverse, which is brilliant as, previously, she had no idea what her feet were doing unless she was going forward very fast in a straight line. Star was so clumsy, she could knock any and every part of her anatomy several times a day! I don't think she had any conception of what shape or size she was or what her body was doing – unless she was running, when she does look stunningly graceful, although not at any other time!

Star's clumsiness did cause me some difficulties getting into the barn, particularly when she stood with her head over the door to the middle barn, waiting for her food. Since she had no idea how to go backward, she effectively blocked the doorway, leaving nowhere near enough room for me to get past her. Horses can be quite unpredictable when circumstances might prove too much, and cause them to react negatively, and because it's still early days, I did not want to squeeze past Star, possibly prompting such a response.

At least the horses are now quite predictable in many other ways. For example, if Charlie tries to get a look in whilst Star is at the gate, he's likely to get a kick, and if Star is desperate for hay and showing signs of frustration, I do not attempt to squeeze past her as I may get bumped.

Working with horses, and, indeed, any animal, is all about not being rigid, and adjusting for the circumstances to make the interaction successful – another of our win-win situations. I know it's widely accepted in horse training that it should be the horse and not us who moves or makes a change, but that approach is neither sensible nor reasonable. For our relationship with our horse to be a true partnership rather than a master and subordinate association, give and take are essential components.

I knew that Star had no idea how to go backward, and I hadn't yet taught her how to do this. She also does not take kindly to people trying to shove her about, so there's little point pushing her chest in the hope that she understands she is supposed to move away from the contact rather than push into it, because she won't.

Fundamentally, how she might react to such a manoeuvre is down to mood and emotion. If she is feeling frustrated, trying to get her to move backward by physical force is likely to result in an overflow of that frustration, and she may push back, or nip. If she is not already frustrated if I try and force her to move back, she may become so, and most likely plant her feet and refuse to move at all.

The solution to this, I've been told, is to place my thumb on the pressure point of her chest and push firmly, whereupon she'll understand that she should move backward.

Actually, all she'll understand it that this hurts! We are told that the horse doesn't feel pain, is being stubborn, or is dominating us – all completely untrue. What has actually happened is that the horse has gone into fight or flight mode, and in this instance is freezing in fear until he has a better idea of what he should do. If I cause Star to feel increasing amounts of pain until such time as she moves backward, she does so not because she

understands she should be moving backward, but to get away from the hurt that I am causing her! The two things are very different.

Besides which, causing pain in order to illicit a response is neither humane nor clever, and certainly not something I would advocate or do. I will teach Star how to go backward using visual and verbal cues, so that she learns the behaviour and the cues for it, rather than learning to avoid pain.

Another problem with teaching horses to move away from pain is that, should they sustain an injury or be unwell and in need of treatment, their conditioned response will be to withdraw, which is not helpful if they need to stand still to be treated. One response to this is to keep the animal still by force: a very unpleasant way to work, and confusing for the horse. How does he know when he should move away from pain, or remain still and suffer it? Many end up in the sad situation of switching off and trying to ignore what is happening to them. Zoning out in this way also makes an animal unreceptive to learning, making training laborious and largely ineffectual.

Unfortunately, force and punishment are used as a means of control, without considering how confusing, demoralising and plain wrong it is to treat our horses – or any animal – in this way. And if training in this way doesn't work, the only direction left to take is one where pain and punishment are increased. This method of working with animals contravenes the Animal Welfare Act, and can never be justified.

So, teaching Star 'back' is undertaken in a positive and rewarding way, and step one is to only initiate training when her frame of mind is calm, and she is not frustrated. If she is frustrated at waiting for her hay, I will throw a small amount to one side of the door, so that she moves away and I can get in. This means that the frustration she feels is not directed at me, and we do not create an association between delivery of food, and me as the source of her frustration.

If Star is calm, I can open the door and hold a small amount of hay at chest level below her

continued page 66

A tale of two horses

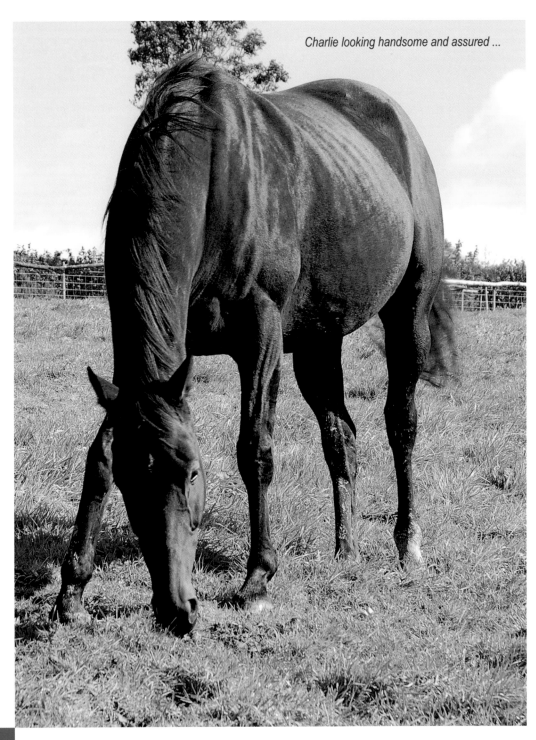

Charlie looking handsome and assured ...

... and Star also appearing content and well.

A tale of two horses

mouth, so that she has to dip her head to reach it. After a few days of this she has decided that it's easier to take a step backward in order to reach the hay: a result, and she's done it all on her own! Now, it's easy to progress this so that she takes two steps back, then three, simply by using this strategy, and once she is going backward easily and without stress, I can add the verbal cue 'back' as she does so. Once she has associated the cue with the movement, I can do away with the hay and add a hand signal, and we have a horse who can walk backward by voice command or hand signal, on her own. (This method can also be employed to give direction to your horse when riding, using only your body and balance.)

To recap, let's go back to how the brain learns, the associations it makes, and the emotional state of our horse.

A horse who is taught in the correct way will learn more easily and quickly than one who isn't. Learning the required behaviour means that this can be applied in different situations, without stress or anxiety: the horse knows his role in the partnership, and this, in itself, makes him feel secure. A secure horse who knows what he is doing is better able to be controlled than one who, despite being attached to a lead rope, or under saddle, hasn't the slightest idea of what it is he is supposed to be doing.

Teaching in such a way that does not cause a horse anxiety or worry around people has other benefits, too, such as him seeking affection and pleasurable experiences like grooming, demonstrating his personality, and developing a bond with his owner.

And speaking of which, both Charlie and Star came to me for grooming today. I didn't do too much, just a gentle brush. Brushing Star first, she began to move about, and I thought she was going to walk off, when, in fact, she was just getting closer for a kiss. Then, when I went over to the post to clean my brush, she came with me!

Charlie did exactly the same as Star: he wanted grooming more than he wanted to eat! He was very happy and made lots of little purring noises!

They're still not keen on having their feet picked up, but neither walks away, now, when I do it. I have been giving them their morning portion of Speedi-Beet® as a reward after we've done the handling, and it's working quite well.

We've been following this routine for the last few days – though not every morning – and it seems as if they look forward to it.

As far as my horses are concerned, we have had their trust for a while now, and they are secure in the knowledge that we will not abuse or scare them, or force them to do something they don't want to do. Whilst they have been happy for us to interact and work with them, they have not previously shown signs of asking for our company. They do purr and nuzzle during and after handling, will come to the barn for breakfast when I call them, and wander around with us when we are in the field, but have not *really* interacted with us.

That all changed today, when both of my horses asked to interact with me when I stopped grooming; another step forward, and one which made me smile all day!

Chapter 8

A big day

It's the beginning of June – officially summer – and it's taken this long for the top field to reach a suitable condition for the horses. The grass has finally grown, and the ground has recovered enough from all the rain we've had this year for the tractor to get on and take a first cut.

And I have had a brainwave! Honestly, I have no idea why this hasn't been thought of before: I'm going to strip cut (alternate rows not cut) the field. This will give the horses a mixture of mature grass and nice, young, fresh grass. It seems the ideal solution for optimum grazing, ensuring a good mix of sugar and starch. It goes without saying that people think I'm mad, but that's been said so often, I've got used to it now.

So, enter stage – or field – left, the tractor. The grass is cut and looks lovely, a bit like an alternative take on a proper stripy country garden, and the next job is to turn the cut grass until it dries, then collect it to store in the barn.

Ahh, first problem: perhaps my idea will turn out to be more of a headache than a brainwave.

The part on the back of the tractor that turns the hay so that it dries properly doesn't so much turn it as kind of spread it about ... not a viable option, I'm told, as it will not stay in the lovely straight lines that have been cut, and, instead, will be all over the nice, knee-high grass that has not been cut. Okay, then, we'll turn and collect it ourselves: how hard can it be, after all?

Several days, many glasses of wine (for medicinal purposes to ease aching backs), and evenings that go by in a fog of complete exhaustion later, we conclude that turning and gathering hay by hand is not one of my better ideas. Once we've recovered from this ordeal, we celebrate Matt's birthday, and I decide that I must pamper him. Not only have I nearly killed him off with my hay plan, but he has also spent the last few months doing whatever was necessary to keep the fields and barn safe and easy for me and the horses to use. And he doesn't even *like* horses (though I'm beginning to suspect he has developed a soft spot for Charlie). After a couple of nice, relaxing days off, it's time to open the summer field for the horses. which they've not yet been in, so it will be interesting to see what they make of it.

Opening the gate, the horses just stand there and look. Some encouraging words from us does not prompt any movement on their part, so I walk into the field to show them there's nothing to worry about, and, sure enough, they follow me in, albeit a little hesitantly. I retreat to the fence to watch them: it's not a good idea to be in the way if they become excited.

It's not long before they're trotting around the edge of the field, clearly doing a perimeter check on their new accommodation, tails high, heads high, and looking at everything. They go round twice. "Well," I ask "what do you think?" They answer me in delighted whinnies as they gallop as fast as they can from one end of the field to the other, then spend the next hour trotting, playing and cantering about, making lots of happy horse noises.

Star relaxes in her summer field. What a hard life ...

The strip cutting has worked a treat, despite nearly killing ourselves in the process. Although advised that the horses would ignore all of the long grass and eat only the shoots, this has not happened. The horses have the ability to choose what their bodies require, and, along with the hedgerows, a small amount of hay that I still provide, and their daily portion of Speedi-Beet®, they are eating a variety of foods, and not just the nice, sweet, green shoots.

Charlie and Star are outside more often than not at this time of year, so there's hardly any mucking out to do, happily, and I can spend the extra time with them. Once I've got my chores done, that is: it's no good if Matt comes home to a messy house and no dinner after a hard day at work!

A CHANGE IN ROUTINE

Charlie and Star are so impressed with their new field that they don't come back to the barn for hay for two days! Their water is in the barn, so they come in for that, but there's no chance of getting them to stay in when they have a lovely field full of grass to eat! Moving into the summer field has upset our usual schedule, but it's easy to compensate for this by changing the routine, as I do want them to continue with the ad hoc feeding that is so good for their hooves and digestive health. The obvious thing for me to do is to take a bucket of feed to them in the field, as they have no intention of coming to me. However, don't be tempted to change your original routine if it's essentially good, as this will create a new regime, which your horse may then come to expect all the time, resulting in having to work to change things back again. So my strategy is to stay with the usual routine, make breakfast and put it out, so that when they do come in for a drink, they may be tempted to eat it, along with a little hay.

This doesn't happen on days one or two, so I don't make it up on day three – there's no point wasting it. I try again on day four. Success. A few days later and they're recalling for breakfast as usual, and coming into the barn if it rains – which it does, frequently. Our routine has been re-established – I just needed to give it a little time.

Many of the dog behaviour cases I see involve an animal who has begun performing an unwanted or inappropriate behaviour that the owners can't cope with. It's usually the case that, rather than this being a new behaviour, it is something that has gradually developed until it becomes a problem. The owners are unaware of this progression, and therefore don't understand why it has happened. When I ask them to look back, they can see the beginnings of the problem behaviour, and realise it has not appeared out of the blue.

A scenario such as this tends to arise out of compensating incorrectly for changes in routine, which gives rise to a new routine and the perceived 'new behaviours' experienced, which are actually existing behaviours that have got progressively worse. This is not to say that we should never change, of course: after all, I did talk earlier about not being rigid, and applying a give and take approach in order to be successful.

If it's been established that a routine is good, then a bit of give and take will keep it successful. Remember that the principles of the routine should be retained, though: for example, I always feed breakfast in the barn, so although I can understand the excitement of a new field and my horses' reluctance to come in, I should not be compensating for this by changing where I feed them.

If a routine is not as good as it might be, improve it by making small adjustments towards what you do want, which should ensure that the change occurs without any fuss at all.

CANINE FOCUS

I'm busy with dog training classes now. Everyone wants their dog to be good at recall, and especially at this time of the year, when the arrival of summer and warm weather means that lots of people are once again taking their dogs out and about, over the moors and to the beach. Unfortunately, recall can be quite a difficult thing for some dogs to learn, and to be effective regular practice is essential to reinforce the new behaviour so that it is not forgotten. Taking our dog somewhere new and asking for recall, when this is not usually done on walks at home, can mean that our dog will ignore us, preferring to have great fun tearing about instead.

The answer? A series of recall and chase workshops.

I begin by telling my clients that if I can achieve recall with my horses, they can definitely do the same with their dogs! Interrupting the chase instinct, however, is a little more difficult to master, and the next step on from recall training. In order to be successful in training behaviour it's essential to establish a good relationship with the dog, horse, or whatever animal you are working with, as none will come voluntarily if they do not have a reason to. So many people go somewhere to walk their dog off the lead, leaving him to entertain and exercise himself without interacting with him in any way until it's time to put the lead back on. Is it any wonder that the dog soon comes to associate his owner and being on the lead with an end to his fun, and therefore decides not to come back when called?

To begin to deal with the recall situation, the first step is to develop a relationship with our dog when we are out. We can have a brilliant relationship at home, but if all we do when out with our dog is look at our mobile phone, then we're not participating in the walk, and our dog is much less likely to listen to us and much more likely to find his own fun.

So, electronic equipment is banned; talking to our dog, playing games and being exciting are the first exercises. Recall training begins in much the same way for horses, but without the exciting bit (I am happy for my dog to be excited around me, but I want my horses to remain calm). Alongside the 'off-lead' fun and games, I also teach 'on-lead' skills, which allows the dog to learn words and movements in a more calm and controlled manner than if he is haring about off-lead. And skills learnt on-lead can be transferred to dogs when they are off-lead, too. Ultimately, without too much effort, the result should be a dog who is off-lead but under control, and able to hear and respond to his owner's cues.

This way of training is a really good strategy for success: teaching outline behaviours (basic directional cues, such as 'this way,' 'let's go,' and recall). It's not important how well these behaviours are performed at the start, as it's about teaching the dog (or horse) the word associations, and an approximate response is sufficient. So, if you say 'this way,' and he doesn't follow straight away, or takes a detour whilst doing so, this is okay, as he is giving the correct response, albeit loosely. These responses can be refined when teaching fine detail behaviours (a faster response; fewer detours) in a controlled environment (such as our garden, or when out on a quiet walk), where there are fewer distractions, enabling our dog to learn more effectively.

This enhances the broader-based behaviours we have already been working on, but now in an environment where we need him to listen to us. It is easier for our dog to perform a familiar action when out in an unfamiliar or exciting place, than it is to teach him an action in an unfamiliar place, with all the distractions there are. So teaching a broad overview behaviour in an unfamiliar place and backing it up with familiar and well learned behaviours that are already established, makes it easier for our dog to be successful.

The same principles apply to horses. In a safe and quiet environment we teach him all of the different movements and actions that he may need to employ when out and about. Once he is happy with these, the next step is to go out on a short walk, and ask him to perform the tasks we have taught him. As carrying out the requested behaviours become commonplace, and not contextually linked

to any particular place or situation, our horse will find it easier to do them when in an unfamiliar place. This gives him a coping strategy, and it will be easier to regain control and his attention, should something unexpected happen.

Going back to dogs, having behaviours in place is essential when we are working with instinct, such as the natural urge to chase. How hard is it going to be for our dog to listen to us when faced with a tempting sheep, who may run away at any moment? Dogs with a strong chase instinct may try and chase the sheep even if she remains still, and even those without such a strong instinct will find sheep exceedingly attractive: trying to get a dog's attention in this instance can range from not easy to almost impossible. So, working at a distance – when our dog is halfway across a field, say –with behaviours that are already familiar to him, makes it much easier for our dog respond to us, occupying his mind with something other than the compelling thought "there's a sheep, there's a sheep, there's a sheep!"

In this way, we are able to get our dog to refocus on us, and do something else, rather than follow his instinct to chase the sheep, and providing him with the very useful tool of impulse control to boot, which prevents the emotional brain from running away with itself, allowing instinct to take over. As we progress, and he is able to make a choice rather than have no option but to chase, we can work closer to the distraction.

Obviously, as prey rather than predator animals, horses will run from rather than chase something, but still the same principles apply: if our horse has a range of familiar and enjoyable behaviours that he can carry out, these can be used to distract and calm him if he is spooked, providing us with the ability to safely manage and get through the situation.

CHOICE – GOOD OR BAD?

Giving an animal a choice – an alternative strategy to the one they are used to using when confronted with things that are either exciting or scary – is good,

of course, but can also create conflict. In the dog's mind, there is a dilemma: does he focus on the sheep (as they are very rewarding), or does he focus on us, as we always have yummy treats (and are therefore also rewarding)?

Assuming that we are working with a contented and well-balanced dog, in the above example, where the dog is at a sufficient distance from the sheep, this is a healthy conflict: we are asking him to use his thinking brain, and not to follow his instinct, when making a decision about what he does. Both options are positive and equally compelling. If we take the dog a lot nearer to the sheep, the balance shifts, and one option – to chase the sheep – becomes more compelling, increasing the likelihood that his chase instinct will kick in.

The same applies to a horse of the same status: the closer we go to the problem, the more unequal becomes the balance, and the more likely it is that the flight instinct will win out, as the horse cannot see another option. Working with a dog or horse who has issues means that the starting point is already out of balance, and if we try and work too closely to the cause of the problem, the balance shifts even further, and the situation becomes something else entirely, and potentially very dangerous.

We see conflict in many situations; often, it will occur when all of the available choices are negative. For example, we want our horse to stand still whilst being clipped, but if the horse finds the clippers very scary, he may try to avoid them by moving away. If the horse is then punished for doing this, it's easy to understand why he perceives his choices as being negative: either endure the scary clippers, or be punished for trying to move away from them! And the reality of such a situation is that he will most probably suffer both consequences, alternately punished and subjected to the clippers until the job is done. This sad and traumatic experience is not going to teach him that he *can* stand calmly, and there is

nothing to worry about: on the contrary, his view that the clippers are very scary will only be reinforced, and he will also come to learn that his owner/handler is scary, too. This situation can give rise to avoidance behaviour, fear aggression, or learned helplessness, where the horse shuts down because none of his options are viable.

Conflict is also seen when available choices are positive and negative, and often occurs when we try getting a dog to do something he doesn't want to by using positive reinforcement. For example, if he's scared of walking under scaffolding, say, we may try to entice him to do so with a food treat. The conflict here is whether or not he is able to ignore his fear sufficiently in order to receive the treat. In some cases the dog may reason "Okay, I want the treat and the scary scaffolding is not that scary," in which case he's likely to be well-balanced and confident. More often, though, we resort to this strategy when a dog is not well-balanced, and has a definite problem with a situation such as this, in which case several outcomes are possible –

- He may make an association between the treat and the scaffolding (which then negates any positive association the reward may have), whereupon it becomes necessary to find something else to use as a reward.
- He may become more reactive to the scaffolding as a result of trying to make him overcome a fear that he simply cannot, which may

progress to a general reactivity in any scary situation, as he did not cope with the last one, and so draws on that same strategy to deal with the next, and the next.

- He may overcome his fears sufficiently to walk under the scaffolding, but will always be wary, and require some help and reassurance in situations he finds challenging.

If we apply this scenario to a horse, there's no positive element, as a common response to baulking at going under or past something is for the rider to kick the horse until he does. Again, it's a choice for the horse to face the scary thing or be punished, and if the horse is not well-balanced and finds situations such as these problematic, the same reaction as with the dog – avoidance or fear aggression, and a heightened reactivity – is the likely outcome.

Working within the parameters of positive reinforcement will make training so much easier, and much more effective, and considerably improve both horse and human safety.

EXCITING TIMES

And if Matt's birthday and the horses moving to their summer field are not reason enough for celebration, we have one more blessing – Norman – our first calf born to us, well, not to us, obviously, but Ruby, his mum. We'd been eagerly awaiting his arrival, and this morning he entered the world, nice and easy with no fuss: a lovely little boy; all black. His dad is a very handsome-looking Aberdeen Angus. Ruby is fine, and seems very content, if a little tired. As if to join in our celebrations the weather has decided to cheer up and the sun is out – at last!

I've entered Star in a postal competition run by British Horse Feeds. I don't think we have any chance of winning, but I'm so enthusiastic and happy, I just wanted to have a go, so keep my fingers crossed. We don't win, unfortunately, but do get a voucher for a free bag of Fibre-Beet®. Excellent.

Off I trot to the local store to pick up the

Proud mum, Ruby, with Norman, her baby.

free gift. Back at home, feeling very pleased with myself, I prepare portions for the horses, and take it in to them. Star eats a little, looks unsure, then tries some more. Charlie sniffs it, has one mouthful, and promptly walks away, closely followed by Star. His expression is a picture: he's absolutely heartbroken that his very favourite food in the whole world has been replaced by something else! I feel very sorry for him and make him up some Speedi-Beet®, which he tucks into straight away, happily snorting to himself.

Now, I know that Charlie is not just being sensitive to a change in food, as I can put any medication he needs in his Speedi-Beet® and he happily eats it. So, I've come to the conclusion that although Fibre-Beet® is just as good, it is not to his liking. No problem, though, we have friends down the road with three lovely horses who will enjoy it.

Remember I mentioned the art exhibition? Well, what a day it was. The set-up team pitched up and began work at 8am, ready for our 10am opening time: the tables were laid out and the easels placed on top ready to receive the paintings. Others began arriving with paintings and cakes, ready to get stuck in. Each painting had to have a note attached to it – its number in the catalogue – and was placed on display. Some helpers were sorting out the kitchen, getting ready to serve tea and cake; some were in the town handling out leaflets and putting signs up so everyone knew we were there. Despite much advance preparation there was still quite a lot of work that couldn't be done until the day, so it took us two hours to get everything ready for opening.

The day went really well, and we had hundreds of people through the doors, which I think the lure of free tea and cake had something to do with! They did stay and look around, though, to be fair. By lunchtime the place was buzzing, and so busy you could hardly move for bodies. It's a very good job we had lots of helpers who made cakes, as we got through a lot more than we had expected to. Things quietened down later in the afternoon, and we closed for a couple of hours prior to our evening private viewing for family and friends, during which time we all went home to get changed into evening wear, and be back at the hall for the last part of the event.

It was a really good show, and so inspiring for everyone to see others enjoying the work produced, and complimenting it. In the end, we sold seven originals, several prints, and 495 cards! All the cakes had been eaten, and I'm sure we got through several gallons of tea! I was ready to head home for a well-deserved rest, and time with the horses.

You may remember I mentioned earlier that I am quite shy, and not very confident, and a good example of this is that I didn't put any of my own work into the exhibition. Writing this book has made me really analyse myself, and I'm beginning to realise how much I could be achieving if I stopped being so worried about failing, or what others might think. I spent months reassuring the art group that their work really was good, and that people would want to buy it. Bit of a contradiction, really, when I wasn't brave enough to show mine, too ...

WORRYING TOO MUCH

It's a lovely – thankfully, dry – morning, the sun is out again, and we're taking Indie for an early stroll. This is so nice … AARRGGHH! Where are the horses? They're gone!

Oh God, oh God, where are they? I panic, and run across the field searching for them, desperately trying not to cry. Has someone stolen them? Have they jumped the fence? Are they dead? By now, Matt is taking over ... he spots them, and they are absolutely fine, laying in the long grass so we can't see them. The relief I feel is HUGE! Charlie and Star look up, give happy nickers, and remain laying down, comfortable and content, whilst I struggle to regain my composure.

I don't know what I'd do if anything should happen to them.

Most early mornings I find them laying comfortably together (I no longer panic when I can't spot them immediately, though it doesn't mean I don't fret), and they don't get up till going on for 9am!

I still worry about them all the time, though, assuming the worst, usually. Why are they out, are they scared to come in, is something wrong? Why are they in, are they ill? Why are they laying down, can't they walk? Why are they standing still, can't they move? Why aren't they grazing? Do their legs look okay? Are their tummies bloated? Am I going to get up one morning and find them on their backs with their legs in the air, either dying or dead? Not nice thoughts, I know, and I am trying to get a grip, but at the moment, I'm over-analysing everything.

I feel that it's just too good to be true, and it can't last. Maybe this *is* just a dream ...?

Chapter 9

Problems, problems …

Well, we're into summer and it's still raining. This has to be the worst summer for ages: the fields are soggy, and everyone is thoroughly fed up with the lack of sunshine.

Charlie and Star have been actively coming over when they see us in the field; following us up and down the fence line more, without being asked, and seem to want to be near when we're about. Many people have dogs around horses, but I don't feel that is right for us, so, instead, we walk Indie in the field the horses are not in, which is why they walk up and down the fence line with us.

Recall is going well; Charlie and Star are responding to my shouts of "Breakfast!" in the morning, and coming in when they hear me, and spy the bucket. Have they learnt to recognise the word, or is this an association with the time of day?

I did say "Come on, breakfast-time" as part of a sentence when we were out the other morning, and Star walked back with me. I did not expect her to pick up on the word within a general sentence, so this is good progress – though it may have been a fluke, of course!

Charlie has become more comfortable and keeps to himself less. He had a massage from Matt and actively leaned into it: when Matt took his hand away, Charlie leaned in for more.

HORMONAL HORSE

They say that bad things come in threes. Well, we have two going on at the moment, so are hoping we don't have to deal with anything else!

The first thing is that Star is struggling to cope with her hormones: she's just come into season, and it has completely thrown her. She doesn't settle at all, and is not letting Charlie anywhere near her – or breakfast and the hay, either! She's also begun kicking in earnest, having discovered that she can turn around and throw her back legs out.

When she's hungry, Star's usual routine is to stand with her head over the door to the middle barn: perhaps she thinks that if she stares at the hay long enough, some will magically appear at her feet! This is where I first taught her to go backwards, as there really is not enough space in the doorway for me, Star, and a bundle of hay. She has been stepping back to let me in for a while now, but not today.

Today is very different, as Star is excitable, moving about a lot and grabbing at the hay: not the usual calm girl who can wait patiently. Basically, she can't think at all, and my requests for her to go backwards so that I can get in fall on deaf ears. Poor girl, she doesn't know what to do with herself.

As has happened a few times since I've had Charlie and Star, I realise I have a choice about how to deal with this –

- Change what I am doing and go round the other way (which is considered a serious error on the part of the trainer for giving in to the horse).
- Stand my ground and do what is necessary to achieve my objective – the generally-approved approach.

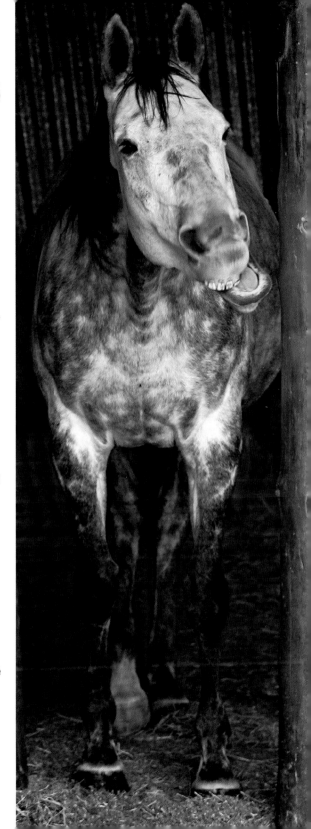

Star is struggling with her hormones.
(Courtesy Andy Francis)

Having read this far, I'm sure you'll know exactly which option I shall choose ... Of course I will ignore what I am 'supposed' to do, and alter what *I* do, leaving Star where she is. The only option, as far as I am concerned, is to go the other way, around the side of the barn, over the gate, and in from the yard.

By now, you will also know why I choose to do this.

The accepted practice of working with horses dictates that the horse – not me – should give way, or she will have gained the upper hand, but, regardless of anything else, at this moment, Star has no intention of going backwards, as her usual reasoning powers are all over the place because of her hormones. And if her brain is not working as it should, we know she will be unable to listen effectively, and will therefore find it very difficult to do as I ask. Even more importantly, as part of her brain is still processing the situation, if I continually ask for something that she does not do, all I will have taught her is that she can ignore me!

In order to comply with established practice, I would have to apply pressure and resort to methods with which I disagree.

Firstly, if I physically push Star back out of the doorway, this is sn involuntary action, which only teaches her that she doesn't need to move unless physically forced to do so. Would this make it more likely that she will voluntarily move the next time? No, she would still be sure her best strategy would be to stay where she was, as she has no motivation of her own to move. And if she chooses not to move, even when I push her (which she obviously has the strength to do), I will be reinforcing her belief that she can resist what is physically being asked of her.

MAINTAINING INTEGRITY

So, what can I do: give up? Yes! Even if established practice says that this will have taught my horse that she is in charge. If I were to continue in the way that a situation such as this is usually handled, I would then have to resort to something other than force, as my strength cannot match hers. Something other than force might involve making things uncomfortable for Star, and if that doesn't work, I would have to make things painful. This approach works by increasing pressure sufficiently so that the horse finds it uncomfortable or painful, and learns to move away from the source of the discomfort or pain. Unfortunately, when horses are adamant that they do not want to move, an ever-increasing amount of force is required each time to achieve the desired result. Taking matters as far as is necessary creates a path that has no end, and no alternative to applying increasing amounts of pain until you achieve the result, or give up.

Coming back to the situation with Star, firstly, she is unable to listen to me in her current emotional state, and, secondly, as she wants to get at the hay, moving backwards takes her further from it. It is quite hard to teach an animal the concept of going away from something in order to have it, and certainly not possible whilst hormonal anarchy rules.

You know, you can almost guarantee that this type of situation is most likely to occur when you are busy, and really don't have time to mess about!

There may be the temptation to give our horse a good shove or slap, or apply pain by pressing on her pressure points, but just think about how this will undermine all of the effort and time spent gaining our horse's trust, and teaching her that we are reliable and predictable. This is an unreasonable way to behave at any time, and has the added danger that, as the survival instinct kicks in, the animal may bite or kick, especially if she is unable to think clearly.

And this will also make our horse more wary of us, so, not only has our frustration caused us to do something that is immoral, our relationship with our horse will have suffered, and we will have to work twice as hard to regain the trust we had before negative methods were used to get what we wanted. An awful lot of consequences result from a single action done without thought, as a means of expediency. Ironically, getting back to the place we were before will require a whole lot more time and effort, and that's one of the reasons I change what I do, and go round the other way.

Charlie sees me, and comes over: "Mmm, hay, thanks, Mum." Star has realised that something is going on behind her, so the doorway is suddenly less interesting. Seeing Charlie eating, she immediately goes to him, nips him on the bum, and steals his hay! Honestly, girls can be so temperamental!

Talking of hay, I have three places to put it in the barn, an arrangement that works well as there is always a choice of direction to go in if one of them sends the other away, reducing any potential stress. Charlie, bless him, is becoming quite laid back, and just moves off to the next pile of hay.

Where food stations are placed can make all the difference.

I spend a couple of minutes talking to Star as she eats. When any animal is hormonal and emotional, there's a tendency to overreact, but by not insisting on doing things in the usual way, and altering my approach instead, I have not given her any cause to react as a result of her raging hormones and emotional state. By softly talking to her I am also reinforcing her perception that I am still the same, whatever else is going on in her head. This is another of my first steps, and one that will give Star the ability to rationalise when in this state, rather than be swept along by emotion, which it what makes the difference between a well-balanced, reliable, safe animal, and an unpredictable, out-of-control, unsafe one. Clearly, this ability is hugely important, particularly when riding our horse at such a time.

SELF-AWARENESS

The same approach applies to us, of course. It takes awareness and self-control to not make a response that is based on emotion, when busy, and our horse is being awkward. Running late, feeling stressed, thinking about what else has to be done, and with no time to do it makes it difficult to even think about using the gentle, patient method I have just described. Yet, becoming more and more frustrated and angry reduces the ability to think clearly, increasing the likelihood of behaviour based on emotion, and not rational thought.

After a frustrating encounter with our horse, if we give in to our frustration, we may go away thinking "Damn, why was he so difficult today, what's got into him, messing me about like that? Well, at least I told him who's boss; he'll think twice next time," but what we do not realise is that our horse comes away from this encounter having learnt that we are unpredictable, and the next time we go into the barn he will be anxious and wary around us. Yes, he may appear quieter (which, unfortunately, reinforces the view that how we behaved was correct), when he is actually keeping his distance until he can determine how we are behaving, and how safe we are. If we're really unlucky, the negative association he's now formed may make him even more difficult to handle as he has absolutely no intention of letting us near him!

The mind is a very complicated thing, and, in this scenario, although we may not be aware of it, we're likely to be a little anxious when we next ask our horse for something, wondering whether he is going to play up again, and approaching the situation with our brain already deciding on action based on what *might* happen, clouding reasoning. This pretty much ensures our behaviour ramps up more quickly

than it did last time: our brain has been here before; frustration is evident, and it knows how to resolve this.

We tend to believe that our actions are based on considered thought, and valid, rational reasoning, but very often they are not, and this is exactly what happens when our horse is in an emotional state. Not everyone responds in this way, of course – some people are able to pause for a minute, suspend emotion, and think before they act – but we are just as liable as other animals to use the emotional area of our brain, and also have the same difficulty checking that emotion to allow rational thought.

If not checked, emotional responses are self-rewarding and become progressively intense: detrimental to our emotional wellbeing, as the most intense expressions of unease and pleasure are despair and mania, neither of which is a healthy emotional state.

Relief from frustration – an emotional response – is the reward element of the behaviour, and as it is self-rewarding, it requires no outside input. The difference in intensity between the two emotional states (relief and frustration) determines how effective a reinforcement this emotion may be. The greater the difference, the greater the reinforcement effect, and the more likely we are to replicate those actions which provided the relief whenever we feel anxious about handling our horse. It's easy to see how the situation can escalate from mild punishment to harsh treatment of a horse whenever he is handled: a very damaging vicious cycle that requires an awareness of how our emotions are fuelling this response in order to break it. We owe it to ourselves – and everyone we come into contact with, human and animal – to increase our self-awareness to prevent being carried away on the tide of our emotions.

BACK TO STAR

More evidence of her unchecked hormones is seen on our last walk of the night with Indie. It's nearly dusk, and this time of the day does have an influence on behaviour. Whilst Matt walks up the hill to check the sheep, Star comes to me for snuggles. Charlie thinks he might like a cuddle, too, and is on his way over when Star runs towards him and begins backing up to kick, successfully moving him across the field for the next few minutes. When not trying to kick him, her tail and head are held high and alert. Charlie doesn't respond; just keeps trotting out of the way, sensible boy.

I call Star's name when she stops her frantic activity for a second to distract her, and, surprisingly, she responds, going against what her instincts are telling her to do, and providing a cue for her to calm down.

Although I have put a tremendous amount of effort into developing the mental abilities of my horses, I did not expect Star to respond to me so quickly, and it shows that the basis is there to enable Star to think through her emotions. I'm trying to give her an awareness of herself, and an ability to think, to work through her emotional state, and not be governed by it. This is the key to developing a well-balanced animal: one who is at the mercy of their emotions, but has the ability to use their rational, thinking mind, even when in an emotional state, to the benefit of themselves and those around them. This is impulse control.

However, I am not trying to suppress Star's emotions, as going down that road is very dangerous in terms of safety, and extremely damaging to an animal's emotional welfare. Neither am I simply trying to prevent undesirable behaviour, because to do so would mean that I am not working with the *cause* of the behaviour, just the *symptom*. Her actions are the outward expression of her underlying internal emotions, and preventing or stopping the behaviour will not change how she feels, in which case, several outcomes are possible.

Our horse may –
- Only be able to prevent the behaviour as long as her emotional state does not escalate. If it does, the eventual physical expression of this will be much more extreme than it would ordinarily have been.
- Find another way of expressing those emotions, which may be worse than the original manifestation.
- Come up with an alternative behaviour to allow her to cope with the stress of not being able to express herself in the way she needs to.

None of the above possible outcomes is healthy or safe.

Rather than trying to subdue her emotional expression, what I need to do is channel Star's emotions so that she uses only safe behaviours to express them. And I need to give her the ability to regulate her emotions so she is not ruled by them, and can still think and behave in a rational way. To teach her to be in control of her emotions I need to work with her brain, and not simply her physical response. Talking to her and getting her to listen to me allows Star to check the emotional turmoil by reasserting her thinking brain in order to listen and respond: an immensely important achievement that allows her to control what is happening inside her brain, rather than be victim to it.

It may sound odd but the starting point to a resolution of this situation is to work from the conclusion of the behaviour, and go backwards to the beginning: a much easier and effective way to work than attempting to tackle things from the start, where an immediate end result is the objective, rather than working towards it in steps.

To illustrate my point, let's take Star's behaviour toward Charlie as our example.

When Charlie approaches, Star backs up and kicks out at him, to keep him away from the resources – in this case, me and cuddles. I'd like Star to be able to cope with Charlie being near her when she is in season, and to only repel him if he is too close and pushing his luck with her. She does not need to keep following him to move him further away from everything he approaches.

If I tackle this head-on by preventing Star from performing this behaviour, I am addressing the start of the issue (her unwanted behaviour), and not really resolving the problem. But how to deal with this? As I've said many times already, I can do this the traditional way, or I can do it my way. The traditional way doesn't teach an alternative, but simply uses methods to halt the unwanted behaviour (kicking) – dealing with the physical expression of the internal emotion. Teaching Star to reassert her thinking brain, to listen to me and go back to grazing, rather than harass Charlie, not only allows her to keep her emotions in check, it also gives her an alternative behaviour – grazing – to occupy her, rather than return to the unwanted behaviour of kicking.

Once these learning elements are established, I can interrupt the vicious cycle that Star is in, and introduce and reinforce the alternative behaviour. From here, I can advance the method in stages, getting to the point where I can interrupt her before she actually begins to kick. The less often she performs this unwanted behaviour the less established it will be, allowing the alternative behaviour to take over.

However, this can only work if Star changes

Happily absorbed in eating his hay, Charlie has no intention of doing as I ask!

her perception of Charlie and the resources. Charlie has no intention of coming too close when she is in season, and keeps out of the way as much as he can. Despite this, Star still feels the need to reinforce the fact that she doesn't want him anywhere near her, or the resources. A combination of hormones working correctly (yes, they really are: when she's not receptive it is natural to repel a male), the newness of their relationship and their home means that she is being a little more forceful than is necessary, but by working with her behaviourally I can help her become more settled, and show her there is no need to respond so strongly. She is able to relax and think rationally despite her raging hormones, rather than be ruled by them, and, along with the ongoing development of the pair's relationship, the desired result of Star letting Charlie know if he pushes his luck, but no longer feeling the need to keep him away from everything, will be achieved.

So, onto the second problem, which is, again, emotional.

IF YOU'RE NOT GOING TO MAKE ME, I'M NOT GOING TO DO IT

We're having a bit of an unsettled time with Charlie at the moment. Since his arrival he's de-stressed, settled down, stopped being so worried, and become quite cuddly. I've worked hard to develop my two horses' awareness of themselves, and let them know that neither force nor physical violence will be used if they don't want to do something.

So far, this has worked well, and they have been happy to go along with most things; if not straight away, then after taking some time to let them see there is nothing to be afraid of.

Well, having acquired some confidence, and a sense of being in control of his own fate, Charlie has come to the logical conclusion that if we're not going to make him do something, then he won't do it! Having given him back his autonomy, he now needs a reason to do things, because, if the decision is left up to him, he won't do anything, as he's quite happy as he is, thank you very much!

A tale of two horses

This is a perfectly natural stage that Charlie is going through, as does every animal and human at some point. What is different is that Charlie's expression of this is somewhat stronger than it would have been had I had him from a young age.

For example, he would *always* have been treated with kind, positive methods, using free will to achieve results, meaning that this stage would have been only a minor hiccup rather than a potential stumbling block. Using a positive strategy enables the development of a strong relationship and bond with the animal. For example our dog, Indie, is perfectly well behaved and happy to do what is asked of him, as this method of teaching has been part of his life from the start, and therefore part of his repertoire of behaviours and routines (he behaves well as that is what he's always done); as part of his personality and part of him.

Obviously, everyone has moments when it's just too difficult to listen, and, of course, we all lose the plot when teenagers! This life stage – a very impressionable one – is very important in terms of how youngsters develop into adults.

In an earlier chapter I mentioned management routines, and not changing one if it's working well. Adjustments to compensate for changes, whilst maintaining the overall structure of the routine, can get us through any difficult times when our horse does not follow what should be his normal and usual practice. The same can be said for behavioural routines. When previously delightful and obedient children become teenagers, it can seem that all we have taught them to date is forgotten, and they become unresponsive, difficult, unpredictable and challenging. Well, it's the case that our horses and dogs go through the very same thing.

Anyone who has brought up adolescents will know how undoubtedly stressful it can be. There seems to be no rhyme nor reason for the unpleasant behaviours that suddenly become commonplace, and frustration, anger, and wanting to tear out our hair are everyday states. It is at this point that we should take a deep breath, count to ten, and do something nice like have a cup of tea and an illicit piece of chocolate to calm down before interacting with our teenager.

How we behave at this point can have a lasting impact on the personality and behaviour of our teenager's adult self.

The complexity of our brain means that a teenager has the option of many possible responses, all vying to be the one that is expressed, and which wins this particular battle depends on how we behave towards our teen when we start a conversation with him; what we do when he doesn't respond as we expect and want, and how we end the interaction. If, at the start, we expect him to be difficult, we are already on the defensive, and less able to listen to what is being said, and even less able to respond in an appropriate manner.

Teenage experiences, and how individuals respond to stimuli partly determine which aspects of their personality are brought to the forefront and which are discarded, shaping their development into adulthood.

This is the very stage that Charlie is going through. Everything he's previously known has been turned on its head, and the resulting emotions are novel and unsettling. Charting his progress, he arrived subdued and opting out of engaging with us; not showing any response to being handled. Then his personality began to emerge, along with anxiety, and he became defensive, and would bite to keep us away. We responded by not pushing things, and therefore not triggering his defences, as a result of which he became quite relaxed and affectionate.

But Charlie was still learning about himself and us, and I actively encouraged him to think and make choices, become self-aware, and let his true personality, likes and dislikes, show. This is such a wonderful thing to do, as it creates a true, honest relationship built on trust and understanding, and also gives an animal a strong sense of self, with the associated confidence to not just cope with life, but truly enjoy it.

A new response? Don't give up!

Charlie has progressed and developed really well,

but the idea is now in his head that he doesn't want to do anything I ask!

Many owners start along the path of building a relationship with their horse based on a kinder way of handling and working with him, but not all are successful in this endeavour, and it is at the point I have just described that some will become stuck, and won't know how to proceed. It is also at this stage that traditionalists will tell them that the problems they are having are only to be expected if they have 'let their animal have the upper hand' ... Feeling that they have no option, some owners reluctantly do revert to the accepted approach to training, and, sadly, the happiness of working in a better way with their horse is quickly lost.

But it's not necessary to do this, as the reason for our horse possibly becoming less rather than more manageable is that we are only partway through the journey, and the trick is to carry on rather than regress. Our horse is learning just as much as we are about this new way: trying out behaviours and giving responses in order to learn from them,

Hmmm, Charlie is quite sure he does not want to do anything I ask him to.

and determine which is the most appropriate to use, trying to understand and make sense of the situation; not pushing boundaries by testing who is in charge.

The difficulty for us is how do we move forward from this point; progress, and come out the other side with a calm, confident, friendly horse who is happy to do as we ask?

Reverting to Charlie: he is behaving like this as I am beginning to ask more of him, and he doesn't feel he has sufficient reason to go along with it, or trust in me sufficiently yet to just do it. Trust takes a long time to develop: that sense of not fully committing – holding something back, just in case – is common to all of us. Some people and animals are never able to trust completely: it's down to the individual, their personality, and the experiences they've had.

I am being more hands-on now, getting the horses comfortable with extra handling and doing what I ask, instead of backing off at the first sign that they're not happy to co-operate. Charlie responds to this in a very definite way by trying to bite me, but, from the point of view of his mental and emotional development, this is a good sign, as it means he is sufficiently self-aware to decide for himself whether or not he likes what is happening: much better than being shut down, as was the case when he arrived. Unfortunately, he has not progressed sufficiently, yet, to lose his learned response, and trust that it will be fine, because he is still too scared to make that leap of faith. But this will come: it's just a matter of time, and responding to him in a way that enables him to make that leap.

Whilst we are in this phase, getting near him is very difficult, but we need to get round this as his feet need doing soon, and an unhappy hoof man and an unhappy horse will be the result if his feet are not looked after properly.

What should I *not* do? Well, certainly there should be no shouting or physical force, or any other form of punishment for not complying. I'm responsible for Charlie's current attitude, and any negative action will undo the last six months' work I've put in teaching him he can trust me.

A tale of two horses

Behaviour is not linear: there are ups, downs, tos, fros, and sideways steps, all of which are normal and not a surprise if we understand why they happen.

So, what *can* I do? Well, behave in a calm, quiet manner, just as I usually do, for a start, and also anticipate his reaction and response so that he does not make contact with me, though stay near enough to him that he knows I'm there, and his attempts to make me go away haven't worked (and that, crucially, he will not suffer any consequences for trying). If I had responded like this when he first arrived, Charlie would not have been able to cope with it, and would have very likely increased the strength of his defence against me if I didn't back away, linking the experience with a negative association. If he didn't become more reactive and less handleable, and we had progressed to his becoming used to allowing me to handle him, the emotion behind the behaviour would be wrong, giving rise to problems further down the line, or if there was reason for Charlie to panic.

However, we are a fair way on from that, and he has learnt that I am always the same, and there is nothing to fear: he just needs to know that this applies in this situation also. Asking more of Charlie makes him uneasy, and I have to find a path through his emotions and behaviour to help him relax and be capable of interrupting this response to offer a different one. Remember, he is testing behaviours in order to learn from them, so my response needs to teach him the right thing; not reinforce his view that he should bite.

My strategy, then, is to stay near, though move away sufficiently so that he cannot actually bite me. Also, to remain calm and focus on doing other things to help defuse the situation. This strategy is clearly not what Charlie expected. I get near him, he snaps at me (though doesn't actually connect) ... then flinches. Hmmm, not quite what I expected, either, but perhaps he has been punished for such behaviour before, and anticipated the same reaction from me. This scenario goes on for a while until he's sure that nothing bad happens to him if he says 'no.'

At least his attempts at biting are reducing, so we're making progress.

A TURN FOR THE WORSE

Not so quick, though! Having determined that I am not going to do anything to him if he chooses not to comply, Charlie gets rather bolshy, and expresses his rebellion in a much stronger manner: biting has progressed to rearing! Lovely! Just what I need, a 450kg horse rearing above me! But this is also not unexpected, and without going into technical detail, I can tell you that behaviour often gets worse when it is about to change for the better. This is called an extinction burst, and the animal makes a last-ditch attempt to hang on to what is familiar and has worked previously before the courage is summoned to stay with the new behaviour being taught. If Charlie has developed properly, this will no longer give the emotional reward that it previously did, and therefore the reinforcement for its continuance is absent, which is what helps him to give up the old behaviour and carry on with the new.

My strategy in dealing with Charlie rearing was the same as with his biting: remain calm; move quickly out of the way; don't focus on him, and behave as if it didn't happen.

His response was astonishing. As soon as his feet were back on the floor he tensed his body (which was angled away from me), and literally jumped out of the way, cringing as he did so, clearly expecting a significant reprisal for his actions. When none was forthcoming he simply stood there, looking confused, so I carried on with a few tasks in the stable, and then left, in the knowledge that there was no point in trying again too soon, as Charlie could begin to default to the behaviour he'd just shown, and stopping his rearing would become much more of a challenge.

Charlie reared again the next day, and, because my response was the same as the day before, I could almost hear his brain whirring, trying to work out what he should do, looking completely flummoxed as if to say, "Well, I have no idea what to do with myself now!" Once he'd got over this he began eating his hay. I stayed for a while – again, not focusing on him – but talking to him softly, telling him he was a clever boy.

Charlie hasn't reared since, other than when he's out in the field playing with Star. A potentially dangerous behaviour was dealt with before it even got started. Charlie is a brilliant boy, and he made that leap of faith. The rearing was only the expression of the underlying reasons for that behaviour, which he successfully overcame.

A FOUNDATION OF TRUST

If tempted to think that my success with Charlie was a fluke, and that problems like this don't usually resolve so quickly, remind yourself of all the work I have put in so far to get to this point. Everything in our story thus far is what has made this possible, and is also the reason I have not been hands-on until now. If I had tried to do this before we'd reached this point in Charlie's emotional development, the problem we encountered may not have been so successfully resolved.

This was obviously not the first time that Charlie had reacted in this way: his initial terror of what I might do to him in response clearly demonstrates this. How well he learned this strategy, I have no idea, but it is possible to stop established behaviours quite quickly if everything associated with that response is different and out of context. He may well have learnt that rearing was an effective strategy in a particular context, but doing so in a completely different situation, with a completely different response to his action, removed the reinforcement for the behaviour. In addition, all of the work I have done with Charlie has given him a good foundation for our relationship, and an ability to think, and not just react. All of these elements were instrumental in preventing this behaviour becoming a problem.

It's still early days, and although Charlie is not always happy to be handled, he is no longer afraid or anxious about it. Nor does he feel the need to do anything other than tell me this by moving his head in a particular way, which I take note of and adjust my handling accordingly so he doesn't worry. This is a good, solid foundation on which to build. We are developing a language where we understand what the other is saying, and know that neither needs to say it in a stronger manner, as we listen and respond to each other.

In order to deal safely and effectively with problem behaviour of this magnitude, it is vital to have an in-depth understanding of behaviour, learning theory, emotions, motivation and reinforcement. It is so important to determine the reason behind the behaviour that is being exhibited. Trying to deal head-on with the kind of behaviour I have described with Charlie is going to put both us and our horse at risk of injury, as well as make matters worse, because, until we understand why our horse is behaving as he is, we won't know what the solution is. Behaviours that appear the same can have a range of different motivations, and it's vital to know what the cause is in order to respond properly, as misinterpretation can lead to an increase in the unwanted behaviour.

The potential for serious injury to us and our horse, and subsequent behavioural problems rather than solutions, is huge if we do not understand what we are doing, and what emotions and motivations we are creating in our horse's mind. Therefore, it might be sensible to enlist the help of an experienced and qualified person. That's not to say you can't work with your own horse, and follow my approach with Charlie and Star, but do so within your knowledge and understanding base, and get sound advice and help when issues arise that are outside of this.

Chapter 10

Leave emotion at the stable door

Something that will make a big difference to the successful development of a relationship with your horse is the consistency and evenness of our mood.

If we behave in the same way each time we interact with our horse, he will come to rely on that behaviour and trust us: a vital component in any relationship, animal or human. Not knowing what mood somebody is in, what may upset them or what they are likely to do, can cause anxiety, and create insecurity and the need for self-preservation, none of which states is conducive to a long-lasting relationship.

A bad mood will be reflected in our behaviour, and could make our horse wary of us, ultimately creating two problems –

One: our horse will be less likely to readily respond or come to us, which may cause frustration – what *is* the reason for his reluctance? – and make our mood even worse. Sensing our uneasy mood – and now our increased frustration – will tell our horse that we can be quite scary, and using stronger tactics to get him to do what we want will only reinforce this.

If this is the case, what we may have failed to realise is that our horse's behaviour is a consequence of *our* behaviour, and what he most needs to allow him to relax and respond to us is for us to be our usual, calm self. This fundamental misunderstanding can be what leads owners to make changes and come up with alternative routines, based on interaction in which they and their horse anticipate problems, and respond based on that assumption ... and so a 'difficult' horse is born.

Two: our horse learns that we are unpredictable, so begins to take more time to assess our mood before he commits to being close to us, resulting in a horse who is always reluctant to do as asked, and slow to respond when he does. Again, this may prompt us to revise our strategy to compensate for what *we* regard as a problem, but which our horse considers is a sensible way to approach us when unsure how we will react ... and so a 'stubborn' horse is born.

However, I appreciate it is often a very difficult thing to leave our emotions at the stable door, as we tend not to realise that we are behaving emotionally until it is pointed out to us, which may not be a welcome observation whilst our brain is locked into emotional and not rational mode. It's only with hindsight that we are able to assess whether how we were feeling had an impact on our attitude and behaviour. Giving more thought to how we are feeling will allow better awareness of our moods, and whether or not our actions are based on logic or emotion – a wonderful technique for moderating and developing our behaviour, allowing us to achieve goals and be successful in whatever we do.

Life is made up of various frustrations – if we didn't have any at all we would probably cease to function, lacking the drive to live – but when things are not in balance our behaviour and moods are usually adversely affected. Managing these frustrations using the logical part of the brain is what allows us to behave in a rational manner rather than go through life as emotional wrecks.

Encouraging positive emotions

We're having the last walk of the evening with Indie. Whilst most people love the summer, I'm a winter person, which I'm told is a bit odd, though the summer does have some benefits, not least of which is that we can go on several evening walks, when Indie likes to run about and play with his frisbees. As a youngster, mornings were his most active time; now he's getting on a bit, and suffers a little from arthritis, our morning walk is usually much more relaxed. He loves to sit out in the sun all day, although, because of the frequent rain, this year has not been a good time to spend in the garden.

The horses also like to play at this time, when it's not yet dusk and the serious grazing begins, and their attention is on things other than grass. Charlie tries to get Star to play, without luck. Appearing to want to run, he takes a couple of steps and then stops, repeating this manoeuvre a few times, adding in a little rearing, but not really getting going. He's tried to motivate Star many times before, but she doesn't seem ready to let go and enjoy herself. Although, these days, she does run for the love of it, she doesn't really interact with Charlie at these times.

Matt and I decide to try an experiment to see if the techniques we use to get the dogs running also work on the horses! You never know until you try, and there's no one about to see us looking daft!

Running with Indie, I call out my usual "Come on, then!" which the horses are very used to hearing, but I do so down at the fence line where Charlie is standing, calling his name at the same time. He seems to want to join in, but I am too slow to run, and it doesn't get him going. Matt takes a turn, and runs much faster than me, making purring noises at Charlie, who responds by snorting! After a fair amount of vocal interaction, Charlie begins to run after Matt, rearing and playing.

Charlie has a good run around the field whilst, on the other side of the fence, we stand and watch. The excitement proves too much for Star and she joins in, running back and forth, as happy snorts from both horses echo across the field.

The last walk of the evening.

Indie with his frisbees. This is his favourite game, and a good way of getting – and holding – his attention.

A tale of two horses

It's fabulous to see the two of them enjoy themselves, and now that they have reached this happy stage it is time to get their teeth done. This can be quite a big deal for a lot of horses (apart from anything else, they have to stand still for quite a while), and if we had tried to do this when they first came to us they may have found the process too traumatic. Our vet, Sarah, Matt and I have decided that, as it is still early days, and they haven't yet developed full trust in us or confidence in themselves, Charlie and Star will be sedated for the procedure.

In preparation I've cleared all traces of food from the barn, and hung the gate that encloses them in the barn, leaving it half open so that they can get in and out. I've also closed the gate to their field, so they are on the yard.

Sarah is lovely. From the start she has embraced my philosophy with Charlie and Star, and is happy to work at their pace rather than pressuring them. The results speak for themselves as they are always easy for her to handle, even though they don't see her very often.

Sarah sets up in the barn, and Star pokes her head round the gate to see what's going on. Star is always curious (whilst Charlie, on the other hand, has seen it all before), and, sensing that something is up, is reluctant to enter the barn. In this situation I can do one of two things: wait for her to come in voluntarily, or force her to. If it is not her decision to enter the barn, she will feel uncomfortable about it; uneasy and anxious to the limit of her tolerance threshold, when she will be compelled to do something to alleviate the situation.

Horses experience exactly the same emotions that we do in situations which are not comfortable for them. The difference here is that we can analyse what's happening, and make a rational decision whether or not to go through with it, whereas our horse – who does not have that same capacity for rational thought – will either have

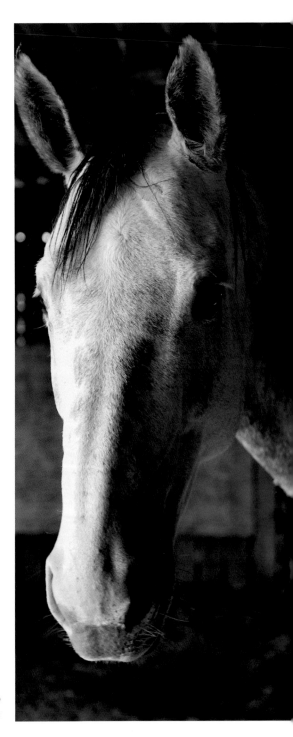

Star must make the decision herself to enter the barn. (Courtesy Andy Francis)

to endure it, or panic and try to escape. And we also have the advantage of choosing not to repeat something we find unpleasant, but a horse has to have his teeth done at least once a year. Imagine just how difficult it will be to get him in the barn the next time if the initial experience causes him to feel nervous and anxious. And if he panics, there's even less chance of a repeat, as the memory of this will be very strong and fixed in his mind. Remember, horses have very good – and long – memories.

So we give Star a few minutes to allow her curiosity to get the better of her, and eventually she comes into the barn of her own accord. There's some anxiety there, as Sarah and her veterinary equipment are not usually in the barn; nor is the gate usually there, but because she has been brave enough to enter the barn, Star's overall mood will be one of self-confidence rather than anxiety, which she has overridden sufficiently. Once in, she explores the equipment, and settles easily. This positive experience results in a calmer emotional state, and a less reactive horse who has not become overly-anxious or panicked, and no horrible memory when the situation occurs again.

It's the last walk of the evening again, and another opportunity to watch Charlie and Star. I still can't believe this is real, and I love them more every time I see them – which is quite a lot! I've even become emotional about them, and I am so not an emotional person. Matt has referred to me as Spock before … I'm just too logical, and, well, always right. Matt knows millions more things than me – he's a truly clever person – yet my logic and common sense usually mean that my assessment of most situations is right, much to his frustration!

Just look at them! Charlie is prancing around the field, really enjoying himself ... Star joins in, and they're off, galloping, rearing and bucking, turning, and running. It's a lovely sight: they've come such a long way from the unhappy, subdued animals who arrived here all those months ago.

Negative emotions

In the previous chapter I talked about how we, as humans, are influenced by our emotions, and the effect they have on our behaviour and actions, and, of course, the same is true for horses. There was a time, long ago, when the study of animal behaviour was not as advanced as it is now, and it was thought that animals did not have emotions, but simply motor patterns devoid of any emotional content, performed for no other reason than physical movement. Further evidence has since proven that, as sentient beings, animals do, of course, have emotions, and very similar ones to our own, although not everyone working in the field of animal behaviour appreciates this, and may not consider how this affects an animal's behaviour.

As far as I can see, understanding the emotions behind behaviour is key to successfully working with animals, and, although Matt will probably not thank me for relating the following story, it nevertheless very aptly demonstrates how we disregard emotion at our peril …

Currently, Charlie and Star are having a portion of Speedi-Beet® in the morning and one in the evening. Star really likes her dinnertime Speedi-Beet®, and usually watches me make it, looking over the rather rustic gate (half of a split stable gate) to the middle barn, which is where I keep the hay and all their things.

Late one afternoon, Matt and I were walking Indie whilst the food was soaking in water to hydrate it. By the time we'd finished our walk it was getting close to dusk – quite an energizing time for horses, as this is when predators begin to appear, the dwindling light makes vision more difficult, and there is an innate desire to have a good feed before it really gets dark. Coming into the middle barn to feed the horses, we could see that Star was displaying signs of frustration; her head still over the gate waiting for her food, rather than munching her hay whilst I prepped her Speedi-Beet®. Approaching their buckets to the side of the gate, she became even more frustrated, displaying increasingly strong signals that quite clearly said she was not coping with the situation.

Matt was not really taking any notice of

A tale of two horses

Star's emotional state, so missed the signals, and went to give her a stroke – a trigger that took Star over her limit. The moment that Matt was in range, she pushed her head forward very quickly, hitting him in the chest with her nose and knocking him off his feet; kicking out at Charlie who was behind her at the same time (both Matt and Charlie sported quite substantial bruises as a result). I did not go near her, but calmly talked to her as I moved to the side of the gate and picked up the buckets. I went into the barn from the other side, leaving the buckets out of sight by the entrance. Still talking softly, I kept my distance, quietly rearranging the hay until she was no longer in the grip of her emotions and had calmed down. I then brought in the Speedi-Beet® and left.

It was emotion that drove Star's behaviour in this instance: anticipation of a food reward, the frustration of waiting for it, and the time of the day all contributed to her emotional state. And she was also in season, which, as mentioned earlier in the book, is a difficult time for Star, so her tolerance threshold is very low. I saw how Star was behaving as soon as we entered the barn, knew she was struggling, and had thought Matt was aware of this, too. If I had realised that he hadn't picked up on it I would have told him not to go near her, and the situation would never have occurred. The best way to defuse highly-charged emotion is not to challenge it, or meet it head-on, as this leaves the horse with no option other than to escalate the emotion – as Matt found out. Repeating phrases she already knows in a calm and reassuring way allows her to come down from her emotional state, and begin thinking in a more rational way.

It's a mistake in a situation such as this to attribute blame: to the horse (Star was only doing what her emotional brain told her to; her action was not premeditated, or calculated, and there was no malicious intent), or to Matt (who was not responsible for the emotions Star was experiencing). But mistakes like this are to be avoided, not least because they can result in serious injury because horses are obviously so much bigger and stronger than are we.

But what, you might ask, if a horse regularly attempts to bite or kick out – is he to blame then?

Horses are not predators, and neither are they aggressors: their preferred course of action if under threat is to flee. So why would they behave like this, and with apparent forethought? Are they, perhaps, 'getting their own back' for something done to them? Many people think so, but this is obviously nonsense.

THE HUMAN PERSPECTIVE

A wonderfully written explanation of how our brain perceives the world around us – and how what we see, hear and believe is not necessarily a true representation of what's happening – can be found in *The Invisible Gorilla and other ways our intuition deceives us*, by Christopher Chabris & Daniel Simons, which is well worth reading, and will provide an understanding of why we do certain things.

Here's an excerpt from the book –
The illusion of cause
... three separate, but interrelated, biases that contribute to the illusion of cause. These biases arise from the fact that our minds are built to detect meaning in patterns, to infer causal relationships from coincidences, and to believe that earlier events cause later ones.

The illusion of cause arises when we see patterns in randomness, and we are most likely to see patterns when we think we understand what is causing them.

With the above in mind, might we believe that something which happened earlier has caused a current event? How often do we see a range of behaviours and think they all part of the same pattern? Or maybe it's the case that we're sure we know what is causing the problems, and that a common factor ties it all together?

In order to make sense of the world and develop understanding, our mind has to make some assumptions in the first instance, and our brain must learn to recognise that a particular group of items, despite differences in shape and size, are still a part of that group. For example, people come

Charlie looking into the middle barn. He's not hormonal – unlike Star! (Courtesy Andy Francis)

A tale of two horses

in all shapes and sizes, but we still recognise each other as people. Recognising that one element of a group of items can look and appear different to others in that group, the brain then looks for patterns – position of the arms, legs, where the eyes are, etc – identifying traits, features and characteristics that confirm commonality of kind.

Our brains are also quick to attribute events to cause and effect – the very basic concept that an action causes a reaction – so look no further for an answer, when, in reality, matters are not that simple. But adoption of this concept makes it easy to understand why we come to the conclusions we do (which are rarely accurate, unfortunately), and why it is certainly easier than analysing information to determine what is actually happening. This is fine, most of the time, as we'd never get through the day or get anything done if our brains analysed our each and every move and experience, but there are occasions where this approach is not helpful, and trying to understand why an animal or human has behaved in a certain way often requires far more in-depth analysis than our brain's initial interpretation. Correct understanding of what is causing a specific behaviour is difficult, and most of us have experienced a situation where we have assumed a reason for an action, and hindsight has shown us that, in fact, it wasn't this at all.

It may surprise you to learn that a horse who regularly bites or kicks does so because he has *learnt* to do so. Our interaction with that horse may or may not have taught him this behaviour in the first place, but will probably have reinforced the behaviour, at the very least. He may not do this every time, and a re-evaluation of the times it does happens may identify that the behaviour is most often seen when we are rushed. We need to think about how we felt and acted at this time, and how our horse responded to this: to what degree did how *we* behave affect how our horse behaved?

UNWANTED BEHAVIOURS: MOTIVATION
AND REINFORCEMENT
Expression of behaviour begins with motivation.

Stimulation of the brain motivates a response, and what form this takes depends on an animal's personality, emotional state, and previous experiences. How this initial reaction is received, and the effect it has, confirms the correctness or otherwise of the action from the horse's point of view, and whether or not he repeats it. A correct response is successful and produces the desired outcome, in which case, the action is reinforced and is likely to be performed again. An incorrect response is not successful and does not produce the desired outcome. The action is therefore not reinforced, and the horse is likely to try something else in place of it.

Taking the example of a horse who attempts to bite when handled, who, somewhere along the way has learnt that he does not like people handling him, as it is not a nice experience. A person walking towards him is the stimulation that motivates the horse to act – attempt to bite – which elicits a response from the person. If this is withdrawal, then, as far as the horse is concerned, his action has been successful: the threat has gone away, providing reinforcement for this behaviour.

However, if the horse's attempts to bite the person do not result in the latter's withdrawal, he deduces that his actions were not successful, and will quite likely try a different approach next time: increase the force of his current action (bite more and harder), bite sooner, walk away to prevent anyone getting close, or kick or rear instead.

By its very nature a lot of equine care is ongoing – grooming, tacking up, and stabling for long periods – and if any or all of these cause anxiety, they will continue to do so unless a change is implemented. In such a situation our horse usually tries to let us know that he is not coping, but if we don't pick up on his signs – and as the source of his stress continues unabated – he becomes ever-more anxious.

Some horses are only just coping with the usual stress and anxiety of daily life, so if something happens that triggers additional stress, undesirable behaviour may be the result. The trigger may be a traumatic experience, but does not need to be a significant event: a simple change in routine, say, which kicks off unwanted behaviour; evidence that the coping threshold of our horse has been exceeded, and he is attempting to communicate his discomfort and distress to us.

For example, a sudden noise which previously alarmed him at the point his bridle was being put on, or perhaps the bit catching his teeth or tongue and causing pain, will mean that he has formed a negative association with this action and that particular piece of tack. The next time he sees the bridle, he tries to avoid it for these reasons, and a behaviour pattern is established, despite the fact that the incident which caused the negative association was a one-off. This is called learned behaviour, and can continue indefinitely. A strategy such as this can be transferred to other things and events that he may find scary, and pretty soon he has learned to respond to any feelings of fear in this particular way. The temporary relief he may experience after performing the behaviour makes him feel better, reinforcing the correctness (from his point of view) of his action. There may also be an additional reward if his behaviour has the effect of preventing his bridle from being put on.

From an owner's point of view, as with other unwanted behaviour, if we give up in our attempts to put on the bridle this only teaches our horse that his behaviour has had the desired effect, and if we tackle the problem head-on, his response is likely to increase in force.

So, what is the solution?

Our emotional brain may tell us to just get on with it; sort it out, once and for all, but this would most definitely be the wrong move. The correct course of action is to go and have a cup of tea, when we can think rationally about how we can help our horse change his perception of the experience that he finds so daunting. The strategies discussed so far should enable the formation of a step-by-step plan to resolve the issue without causing either horse or owner further fear or anxiety, ensuring the safety of both.

We should leave emotion at the stable door, and focus solely on the task in hand to avoid missing important signals that our horse may be giving out, to prevent problems like those we've discussed in this chapter, and to keep all concerned safe.

VISIT HUBBLE AND HATTIE ON THE WEB:
WWW.HUBBLEANDHATTIE.COM · WWW.HUBBLEANDHATTIE.BLOGSPOT.CO.UK· DETAILS OF ALL BOOKS
· SPECIAL OFFERS · NEWSLETTER · NEW BOOK NEWS

91

Chapter 11
Do unto others ...

A lovely sentiment, and one I endeavour to adhere to, as I think it's the right way to live: to give others a chance to show that they are decent and honest, until and if such time they show that they are not. Matt, however, doesn't agree: he thinks that abiding by this ethos makes me 'too nice,' and leaves me open to exploitation. Whilst I don't believe you can ever be too nice, he is right about my being exploited, as, unfortunately, not everyone lives by this sentiment, and if I am not careful my good nature can be taken advantage of. But by taking time to understand another's intent, I hope to avoid being taken for a ride.

What has this got to do with horses? I hear you ask. Simply this: I apply the same principle to my relationship with *my* horses, and also to how I work with other horses and animals. When treated with compassion and respect rather than violence and intimidation, our horses can achieve wonderful things, and will also develop a lovely, balanced nature.

I find it completely baffling that, throughout his life, Charlie has been discarded time and again, because he has apparently been considered useless and worthless. It's incomprehensible to me that no-one has seen how wonderful he really is, and I wonder why this is.

Thinking about it, though, perhaps the following are a few possible reasons –

- The Thoroughbred reputation.
- Previous owners' experiences.

- A tendency to perceive a relationship based on previous experience with a particular breed.
- Intractability – doing things as they have always been done, without question.
- The inability to recognise that there is a sound reason behind all horse behaviour.

Preconceived perceptions can influence our actions, and are sometimes the reason why many Thoroughbreds are taken on, only to require rehoming when their owners are unable to manage them. The same can also apply to any breed, of course, but owning an ex-racehorse has become more popular, and I see more adverts that begin with 'Wonderful Thoroughbred looking for new home, through no fault of his own' than those for other breeds.

In general terms, how we treat our horses, and the methods we use when working and training them, is somewhat behind the methods used to handle our dogs. Thankfully, there are notable exceptions to this, but also – sadly – examples of backward thinking that are even worse; generally, this is where we are as a nation.

Is it right to treat animals with violence? It sounds like such a harsh word, doesn't it? and makes right-thinking people want to shy away from the notion. But it's a subject that needs to be addressed. What would *you* think if you brought your puppy to my training class, and I smacked him if he didn't do what I wanted; shouted at him for performing a behaviour that wasn't asked for, or yanked on his lead to make him follow me? I'm sure you'd think my actions unnecessarily harsh, and my teaching methods very poor ... but would you consider them violent? Amazingly, many trainers do not.

These days, if this style of training is used for our dogs we let it be known that is is unacceptable, and do not allow them to be mistreated in this way. But what about if our *horse* is on the receiving end of violence and force, the level of which is usually stronger than that used for a dog? If a horse does not understand and makes mistakes, the whip or stick may be used, and with ever-increasing force. We press their pressure points, pushing harder and harder to make them move, and some cruel individuals even hit, punch or kick with all their strength – which I have been unfortunate enough to witness. Quite simply, using pain and force to attempt to get an animal to do as we want can never be right.

Human beings are complicated and complex animals: kind, compassionate, inspiring, caring, nurturing, funny and happy on the one hand, but with the capacity, in some cases, to inflict pain and suffering. And one of the reasons for this is that relieving frustration is self-rewarding – it makes us feel better – and the more frustrated we feel, the greater the relief when something is done about it. As much as we would like to believe that the majority of people would not inflict unnecessary pain, the sad and sobering fact is that a good proportion do.

The emotions and drives involved in doing so are complicated and addictive, and the unhealthy cycle of self-reward and punishment is worse when directed at other animals. Whereas we might be able to restrain ourselves when interacting with another person, very often, animals are not viewed in the same way. There's a widely-held belief that animals exist purely for us to use as we wish; without any right to a life of their own. But, of course, they are not machines to be switched on and off at will, performing precisely the same way each time, but living, breathing, *feeling* beings, with lives of their own that they want to live, free from fear, pain and suffering.

LIMITING OPTIONS

And there's another, very important, consideration to going down this path, which is: where do we go from there? If we use force in an effort to make our horse comply, what do we do if he doesn't? Back down, and let it go? For most, this will not be an option, as it will be considered that the horse has 'won.' No, the unfortunate consequence of a situation such as this is that more and greater strength force will be used in an effort to alleviate the feelings of frustration that the perpetrator is experiencing.

And what is learnt from such a traumatic event? Well, the horse will certainly learn that he is likely to suffer physical violence, and, as a result, may well prove even more difficult the next time in an effort to protect himself. And our lesson? Even though we don't know why our horse is being difficult, we decide that he needs to learn to submit to our wishes, and getting him to do so in whatever way is necessary teaches him 'who's boss.' It's fairly evident that, in this situation, we and our horse are talking completely different languages, with no understanding of what the other is saying ...

I would love to say that the foregoing is an imaginary scenario, but, unfortunately it is all too real and very common. Whilst we have worked very hard to increase standards of welfare and training for our dogs, the same cannot be said for our horses, and so many are suffering sustained abuse on a daily basis due to a lack of knowledge of their natural behaviour: how they learn, and the impact their emotional mind has on their behaviour. Many who train horses do so without bringing themselves up-to-date with what is scientifically proven, and ethically correct. The irony here is that, with a basic understanding of the important links between behaviour and the emotional mind, training can be far more effective and efficient, achieve better results, and really provide a horse with a solid foundation.

Sadly, many trainers and owners do not see

anything wrong with treating horses with violence, and this is the crux of the problem. So many people use the word 'respect' when talking about handling and working with horses, but respect is not at all evident in the way that they work. A horse who is subjected to cruelty and pain when being trained is not in the least bit respected, and that old adage 'being cruel to be kind' is way off base in this context.

How many who work in this way have a true awareness of what they are doing, and the impact it has on the horse? Not all of those who work with horses have the necessary knowledge to understand the behavioural and emotional implications, but still must have – however much they might choose to ignore it – an understanding that they are being physically violent to another sentient creature.

There is no excuse for those who claim to be professionals using methods and techniques that were disproved and became obsolete years ago. In any other industry this would be completely unacceptable: a solicitor, say, who hadn't done anything about keeping up-to-date with current law, would be no use at all. Why should it be any different for a horse trainer?

The following are some of the objectives and methods used currently to train horses.

What do you think about them ...?

- TEACHING AND REINFORCING PERCEIVED HELPLESSNESS

This method teaches horses that they cannot do anything of their own free will, thereby undermining their self-confidence – and there are a lot of horses with confidence issues.

- SUBJUGATING A HORSE'S PERSONALITY

Reinforcing obeyance of our will at all times; drumming it in that it is not acceptable to try and avoid compliance, even when it causes discomfort, pain or fear. Treating any animal like a machine, without desires and wants of their own, can only lead to problems. As prey animals, horses will submit rather than fight, and teaching perceived helplessness has accentuated this behaviour: one of

the reasons why it's possible to abuse them to such an extent, and why people suffer far fewer injuries than might be expected. But when things do go wrong, they often do so on a large scale, with resultant serious injuries, and who can really blame the horse if that is the case?

- USING FEAR AND PAIN TO ACHIEVE RESULTS

Why can't we use positive motivation to train our animals? Why is some training based on negative reinforcement – the 'This is horrible, but it will be even more horrible if you don't do what is wanted' school of thought? For the horse, all options lead to the same traumatic outcome, so what's in it for him?

- MANIPULATING ALL OF THE NEGATIVE ASPECTS OF A HORSE'S INSTINCTS AND BEHAVIOUR (LEARNED HELPLESSNESS, THE USE OF FORCE, ETC)

Exploiting vulnerability is a quick and easy fix for ourselves, saving us the time that's needed to do things properly. It's a very short-sighted view, and provides no contingency for when things go wrong ... as they inevitably will.

Shouldn't we demand that those people who handle our horses do so without causing fear, pain and suffering? Better and kinder methods would be –

- Not yanking on lead ropes with increasing force if the horse does not do what is asked.

- Not using the whip to force compliance when yanking does not work.

- Ensuring that trainers understand why aids should be used as tools rather than solutions.

- Allow enough time and effort to ensure the horse can understand what is being asked of him.

- Base training on positive reinforcement methods that promote enjoyment and a willingness to learn.

- Ensure trainers and handlers possess a minimum level of competence, be up-to-date with current scientifically and ethically sound theories and methods, and understand the effects their methods have.

RAISING STANDARDS

I expect better for my own and all horses, and could cry when I think of how unhappy, sad, and scared many horses are for most of their lives – which is how Charlie and Star might have been. Obviously, I think that being with me provides them with the best possible home, and although there are many, many great homes out there, they may well have ended up in one of the those where they were not treated well.

It's also important to keep in mind how unbalanced, unhappy and reactive my two horses were when they arrived. If Charlie and Star had found themselves in a home that used the all-too-common, out of date handling and training methods I've described, they would either have become subdued, their wills broken, leading sad, unhappy lives void of any enjoyment, or may have become reactive to their mistreatment; then passed on to those with a reputation for dealing with 'difficult' horses (which translates to the next person being harsher than the last). How long would this carry on, I wonder, before they were deemed unmanageable, and put down or sent to market for the meat trade?

Luckily, many horses do not go through this experience, but it does happen. Many won't suffer this level of abuse, but a great many are abused to some extent on a daily basis.

As sensible, sensitive people we are fully aware of what we do and the repercussions of our actions, with the ability to choose to do things the right way, with compassion and respect. Happily, modern methods and a growing awareness mean that many more owners are choosing to work with handlers and trainers who employ kind methods, and who will take the time to demonstrate what is possible, providing us with the inspiration to learn how to work in a better way with our horse.

The idea that there is nothing wrong with subjecting horses to pain, fear, abuse and bullying is plainly erroneous. Accompanying that with completely inappropriate environmental conditions such as stabling animals with very little or no turn-out or exercise, or in isolation, because that's how it's always been done, simply compounds the problem. It is our responsibility to say 'Enough!' and demand that cruel, outdated methods of training be forever consigned to history, in order to give our horses the level of welfare they deserve.

A BETTER WAY

So, enough about those who work in a negative way with their animals. Let's think about the possibilities we create when we work in a positive way.

I have no idea where Charlie and Star will take me with their training; we have yet to determine what they like doing best. I know Charlie does *like* doing things – to think, for example – and is developing quite a playful aspect to his personality, so maybe agility will suit him best. Star loves to run, and I suspect that her favourite thing to do might well turn out to be hacking, when she can have a really good gallop. We'll see: the possibilities are endless; they have so much potential they can be whatever they want to be.

This is the beauty of working in a way that allows your animals to develop and grow, providing the freedom to make their own decisions and express preferences. Charlie and Star know best what they are really good at, and what they enjoy; I'm giving them the means by which to tell me. And if that isn't reward enough, it's a fact that an animal trained by positive reinforcement is far safer and more reliable to be around. There's no valid argument for continuing to train using negative reinforcement and punishment.

Personal development is essential to the psychological and emotional welfare of ALL animals, and not just people: how else will they learn and develop to be the best they can?

Training should be a big part of any horse's or dog's life. Everything we do from teaching boundaries, to play, to movement, is a form of

A tale of two horses

Preparing for a play session with Charlie and Star. Such a lot can be learnt through play.

training. Just as we continue to learn throughout our lives, so, too, do all animals. Teaching them how to understand, interpret and react to new situations is not only rewarding to them, it also provides the tools they need to behave appropriately, and without undue anxiety or stress.

The best way to teach your horse is by employing the win-win approach I talked about earlier, which is so easy to do.

● DECIDE WHAT YOU ARE GOING TO TEACH
There is no point in working your horse without an objective, as he will struggle to understand what it is you want and may do the wrong thing.

● BREAK TRAINING INTO SMALL, MANAGEABLE STEPS
All behaviours and movements can be broken down into steps that make learning easy, and get you from A to B without difficulty. Remember how earlier I talked about my future goals for Charlie and Star, and how I intend to achieve these.

● TEACH EACH STEP UNTIL YOU ARE SURE IT HAS BEEN PROPERLY LEARNT; ONLY THEN MOVE ON TO THE NEXT
Each step should consist of the perfect example of what you are teaching. So, if you are teaching your horse to wait and not mug you for his treat, then you need to teach him this until he is calmly waiting with his head in a position you would like, maybe looking

forward. If you are at the stage where he can wait, but he is finding it hard to keep his nose away from the treats, you are not ready to move on yet. Moving on before he has learnt the step correctly will mean that things fall apart later.

- IF YOUR HORSE DOES NOT UNDERSTAND, MAKE IT EASIER FOR HIM TO DO SO

How many steps are there from A to B? As many as are necessary for your horse to understand what's being asked of him. Break down the steps to allow him to do this.

Remember, win-win, which means that both you and your horse should regard training as a good thing, and take away something positive from it. It also means that if you make each training session a pleasant and successful time for your horse, he will always be happy to try things, behave well, and do as you ask.

Indie is a perfect example of this. He doesn't understand how to be naughty, or ignore me and not come back when we are out; to take something he's not supposed to; to go where I tell him not to. Since he arrived at nine weeks old we have been training; every single point has a purpose. To Indie it is just fun and play, with some concentration and new experiences, but everything I teach him is instrumental in making Indie capable of looking after himself, be reliable, and also happy. I do not run around after him all day trying to prevent his getting into trouble, or doing what he shouldn't: he simply doesn't do those things.

And the magic ingredient? Win-win training.

The reason Indie is always successful is because I adjust his training so that he doesn't fail. If something is too difficult for him I make it easier; if something is not understood, we try a different way. And if Indie's mind is not on the task in hand, or it seems he might be interested in something I don't want him to be interested in, I'll do something that makes him wag his tail and focus on me. Indie has grown up with no idea of how to change his behaviour to avoid me, sneak about, or do his own thing when I am not looking, which is what so

many dogs do. It simply is not in his repertoire of behaviour, and nothing he has ever experienced, so he simply hasn't learned to do it.

Obviously, I have had the opportunity to train Indie in this way for most of his life, apart from those first nine weeks when he was with his mum, but it's never too late to begin training. If unwanted behaviours have become established, teaching those that you do want should allow them, in time, to gradually replace the unwanted behaviour.

ADJUSTING FOR SUCCESS

I get some surprised-looking clients when I say that if our horses don't understand what it is we are asking, or do the wrong thing, this is our fault and not theirs, but it's true. As his teacher, if our horse does something different to what we ask of him, we need to determine why that is, and correct or adjust our approach. (I'm assuming that, as you've read this far into my book, you do not subscribe to the outdated and erroneous notion that adjusting your behaviour will allow your horse to be dominant, and take advantage of you.) Let's consider how our behaviour might affect our animal –

- HAVE I BEEN UNCLEAR?

Just because *we* know what we are attempting to communicate to our horse, it does not mean that we are doing this in a way that our horse understands.

- HAVE I CHANGED THE CONTEXT?

What a horse understands and is able to do in one place does not automatically translate to another. Learning takes in not only the actual movement or action, but also the environment, and where *we* might be positioned, or even what we are wearing, and what else happens in conjunction with that particular behaviour.

- HAVE I ASKED FOR SOMETHING HE DOESN'T KNOW HOW TO DO?

A horse cannot read minds, so expecting him to do something he hasn't been taught will obviously end in failure.

A tale of two horses

- HAVE I ASKED FOR SOMETHING WHEN HIS ATTENTION IS NOT ON ME?

One of the most common problems I see. There's little point talking to someone if they are not listening to you, so why do we do it with our animals? Get the attention, get the behaviour.

- HAVE I ASKED FOR SOMETHING THAT MY HORSE MAY FIND DIFFICULT TO DO IN THE PRESENT CIRCUMSTANCES?

Has something which has spooked our horse whilst out hacking made him anxious, worried, or scared? In which case, listening and learning is more difficult for him when in this state.

Interrupt or distract wrong actions, and encourage and positively reinforce correct ones. You are communicating a message: you've tried that, now try this. Praise him for doing it, and, as you progress, anticipate and prevent those behaviours you don't want before they happen. Make training and learning pleasurable, and never reprimand your horse, because if he is scared to try things, he won't offer you alternative behaviours.

Treat your horse as you would like to be treated. How well do you think you would learn new things if your boss was always shouting at you? You'd probably be wary about trying anything in case it set him off, and may not even listen to him properly. Your horse is no different: he will give you his best if you give him yours.

Approaching training with this ethos in mind allows the all-important win-win situation to occur. Your training will be effective, and you will develop a stronger bond with your horse, gaining a happier, more content companion at the same time.

CONVERSATION AS EDUCATION

Do you talk to your horse? Maybe, like me, you do so as a way of putting your thoughts into words: what to have for dinner; how nice it would be to stay home and not have to go to work! I'm constantly talking to my two – and Indie – and this forms an essential part of their learning and development, as talking to your horse is not just conversation, it's education.

Most of what I say has a meaning, and teaches something. I tell them what I'm doing, for example; where I'm going; the names of things; a running commentary on what they are doing (turning right, walking down the lane, etc). It's not long before they come to recognise the same, often-spoken words, and associate them with what they are seeing, or the activities they are doing.

Indie's perfect behaviour is only half due to specific training, such as sit, recall, leave it, etc, and the other half is down to talking. If you have a dog, a good experiment is to grab a pen and paper, and note down everything he does in a day, and the times he spends doing these, and you'll immediately see that the time spent in specific behaviours such as responding to 'sit' involves a very small portion of his day. With Indie, I spend the rest of the time talking to him as a means of training and learning.

Now apply the same exercise to your horse, and ask yourself, does he know the names of everything around him and in his environment? Do I have to lead him and manage him, or can I direct him and he understands me?

Indie knows the difference between the garage, the shed, and the barn, so if I ask him to find his dad, he may first look in the garden, but, if he can't see him, I tell him where Matt is and off he goes. This type of learning is as important as many of the specific behaviours we'd like our animals to learn: I have so much control of the situation and all I'm doing is talking to Indie.

And guess what else this does? It promotes self-confidence in an animal; the ability to understand and be aware of what he is doing, what is happening, and where he is going – an ability we need to promote in our horses who, as prey animals, don't naturally have an abundance of self-confidence. How easy and comforting it would be for them if they were able to appreciate and understand that they were going down the lane to the corner to see the sheep, and then home. I know it may sound like an unusual way of training, but it works. If they know where they are going they don't have any anxiety about it.

APPLYING CONVERSATIONAL APPLICATIONS

Matt, wonderful husband that he is, has been doing much work to get the barn to a state where it doesn't look as if it wants to fall over in an exhausted heap, and also has a few DIY projects on the go. Before I go further it's relevant to mention that Matt is far from quiet when working: things bang, crash, fall with a thump, and there may, possibly, be the occasional exclamation when things don't go to plan. Matt has a back injury, and, as anyone with a bad back knows, everything falls on the floor, so, there's always a lot of crashing and thumping.

Anyway, two reactive horses who are still fairly new to the environment definitely do not appreciate the noise that Matt makes: they startle, and then leave the barn (how quickly depends on how much and what type of noise Matt is making).

In order to make such a situation easier for Charlie and Star, I've been teaching them ways to cope. Firstly, I have taught them to recognise the word 'dad.' Every time Matt comes into the barn I tell them "Look! Here's your dad," and they know this very well now, and look for him whenever I say that word.

The next step is to teach them that the noise is coming from dad: if they can understand that the noise is not a threat, they won't feel the need to react to it. When Matt's working I go into the barn and tell them "It's only your dad, making that noise," and gradually we have gone from their startling and leaving the barn to the point where I can tell them, just before he does, that dad is going to be making a noise, and they don't startle at all, but simply look up. I tell them "Yes, it's just dad working," and they go back to eating, completely unconcerned. They no longer react to noises around the farm at all, even those which are different and inconsistent. In fact, the last job Matt did the pair of them stayed and 'helped,' although I'm not entirely sure that Matt considered it *was* help …

Of course, perhaps if I had just left the horses to it they might have got used to the various noises in their own time, but the point here is that this was another of my 'first steps,' letting the horses

know that the noise was not a threat, so no negative emotional aspect attached to it. Getting used to it on their own might mean that they would always dislike noise, and whilst they might be able to cope with this in a familiar, reassuring environment, how much worse might it seem, and how much more anxious might they be when subjected to it in a strange, possible scary, environment, which might also escalate and cause additional problems.

My point is that the way that Charlie and Star have learnt not to fear noise of any kind makes its acceptance transferable to other situations. And even if they do react I can reassure them by telling them the familiar words: "It's okay, dad's making a noise," which they are able to relate to and apply their coping strategy because this is how the brain engages coping strategies, I'm just giving them a helping hand.

The socialisation period that occurs in the early part of the life of every animal is when the brain is most receptive to new things. At this time, animals will explore everything around them, apparently without fear, and interacting with all kinds of things, which, as they are unknown, don't have emotional or physical responses associated with them. What happens in the course of this interaction determines what associations are made, and how the animal in question behaves in later life. Stored as memories, the brain refers to these associations in the future to decide how to deal with a current situation. This is what a coping strategy is.

An animal who has been denied the chance to explore and learn is ill-equipped to cope with life, and usually has significant behavioural issues as he matures, because he has no coping strategies; there is nothing to draw upon about how to deal with whatever situation he finds himself in.

By teaching Charlie and Star positive associations and emotions that enable them to develop extra coping strategies for things and situations they find difficult, or don't know how to deal with, I am providing the equivalent of self-learned coping strategies. Then, when we come across a similar situation somewhere else, I use the appropriate phrase as a cue to allow the horses to select and bring to mind a particular coping strategy.

Developing coping strategies with animals who need help involves providing an alternative, acceptable behaviour to the – possibly undesirable – one they currently perform. Strategies which are based on word association are designed to recall a feeling; an emotion, rather than a course of action. Once that emotion is present, it diverts focus from the situation that's bothering them, and I can then ask for certain action behaviours to get us through it.

Different situations require different approaches and different coping strategies: whether I use action, words or a combination of both is dependent on the situation.

Star is curious about what Matt is doing, and wants to be involved!

Chapter 12

Foundations, foundations, foundations!

It's September, and a bit on the chilly side. Having rained pretty much all year, it doesn't look as though it's going to stop any time soon.

Norman, our calf, is doing well: although only a couple of months old, he's put on good growth. His mum, Ruby, is happy, and his Auntie Strawberry is helping look after him, too.

Star has struggled with her seasons, and the summer has been very difficult for her, so I hope she settles down a bit as it gets colder. Charlie has become very adept at getting out of her way when she's hormonal, and my input is now minimal, which is a good improvement.

This evening Matt came into the barn with me. He comes in quite often to see Charlie and Star, but he's a little scared of horses, and Star's episode earlier in the year has not exactly helped him feel more relaxed around them. It comes down to being able to correctly read their body language, and understand the emotional aspect of their moods. If unable to gauge how they are feeling, and what their intentions are when they move and interact, Matt will remain wary of them, keeping his distance to talk to them, offering his hand for a stroke if they are calm and still. Very sensible.

You may remember I talked previously about how we assume we automatically have a relationship with a new horse, when actually we don't know them at all (although what we might have, of course, is a general overview of horses and how to handle them). Body language is a very interesting thing: generally speaking, the same postures in the same species mean the same thing, although, as mentioned a few times so far, nothing is ever quite that simple!

For example, two horses can display the same posture, but, depending on context, the meaning can be different for each one, which is where emotion comes in, as it is this that lends body language its intent. If we can't distinguish between the same expressions of movement, we do not understand the motivation behind it, and if we don't understand this, we can't know the likely impact our behaviour might have on the horse, and the subsequent outcome. This is where mistakes are made and people and horses get injured, because we have an enhanced perception of our ability to read the horse, when the reality is that we simply cannot fully understand and interpret a horse's body language until we have built a relationship with him, and know him well.

I know exactly how to behave around animals – I do it for a living – but I do not try to interact with them until I know their personalities, and what might cause them to become anxious or afraid. Sometimes, clients think that as I work with animals I will handle and stroke them from the moment I arrive; not if I want my limbs to remain intact and firmly attached to my body, I won't!

DON'T RUSH IN

Not long ago I met a dog who was terrified of Wellington boots, although, of course, had no way of knowing that this dog found them terrifying, and would feel the need to defend himself if they got

A tale of two horses

too close to him. As this is my profession and I am comfortable around strange dogs, many assume that I always say hello to a new dog, but I do the exact opposite, minimising everything I do in order to be as innocuous and non-threatening as possible, which reduces any risk to me, and prevents triggerng any behaviours that the animal is having problems with. Should the latter happen, I may not know how to respond, and, more importantly, it means that the animal has felt the need to defend himself against me, which is not a good start when I am hoping to gain his trust sufficiently to at least be around him, even if not hands-on. So I did not try and interact with the welly-fearing dog, which, when she saw my footwear, the owner was relieved about, and the dog had no reason to fear me. Discarding the offending footwear, I worked in trainers – and resultant wet feet!

Meeting new animals I initially make an assessment of their behaviour, emotional state, and motivation in order to understand what is going on, and only then can I suggest a course of action that will improve the particular situation. In the couple of hours that I have there's not time to build a relationship, but I am able to make an assessment by looking not just at the symptoms (the 'presenting behaviour'), but also everything leading up to these, and everything after, along with the animal's lifestyle and environment. The owner provides me with details of their animal's personality, and specific questioning allows me to tie together the elements to understand each animal.

Returning to Matt and his interaction with Charlie and Star, he has been very careful and quiet in the barn; not trying to get close to them. Charlie has a history of mistreatment, and Matt is scared of him. Actually, Charlie is scared, too, which means that each has been wary of the other, and have taken things very slowly.

Tonight was a step forward: Charlie asked Matt to rub his head. Charlie really likes having his face rubbed, but doing so means that his teeth are a bit too close to Matt for him to be comfortable, so he moved to the side and Charlie leaned into him.

A nice massage ensued – a big deal for Charlie to let down his defences and not become anxious – and Matt was also reassured and less scared. This was obviously a positive encounter for both of them.

Star has started to follow me and mirror my movements. Approaching me when I walked over to the fence after taking off her rug, she followed when I walked away. I stopped; so did she. I continued and she again followed. She did the same thing a couple of days ago, though can take only a few steps before becoming worried. But this is fine: Star has gone from a reactive horse who walked away the moment you went near her to one who wants my company, albeit somewhat tentatively.

It's so good to see them both progressing and developing, reasurring us all, people and horses, that these are good relationships we are building.

TEACHING SELF-AWARENESS

The weather has not really improved all summer, and now it's not just wet, but getting cold, too. Wet, cold horses are not very comfortable horses, so, I am teaching the two of them to be self-aware and stay comfortable, which, unfortunately for me, necessitates going outside every time the weather is bad and getting them to come into the barn. But, as I want Charlie and Star to be aware of how they feel and able to manage themselves, simply putting a headcollar on each and leading them into the barn only teaches them to follow me, and not to act independently.

The first step is to call them, and get them to walk over to the barn with me, but this is not as easy as it sounds. You'd think that they would have half an ear cocked, listening for all sorts of noises, but not so, it seems, and, at the moment, they are zoning out and enduring the weather whenever I go out. So, the first step is actually to get them to hear me call them, and I have to get quite close for this, though when they do realise I am there, they look surprised! I'm getting very wet traipsing across the field to get their attention, and getting them to follow me back to the barn has not been exactly successful either. I'm wet and cold, and missing my dinner to do this!

Zoning out – when eating, horses are often not interested in listening or responding. (Courtesy Andy Francis)

I expect Matt will be enjoying a glass of wine – hope there's some left for me when I eventually get in!

The horses are also wet and cold, and, although, no doubt, wondering what on earth I am doing, are not following me in as I want them to. Time to use my secret weapon: a bucket of Speedi-Beet®. Surely they can't resist this? Yippee, success! Two horses now in the barn, feeling very pleased with a bucket of their favourite food, which they never usually get at this time of day.

And so go the next few weeks: a seemingly endless round of walking across the field to get their attention, walking back to the barn, fulsomely praising them before being able to go back inside to dry yet another set of clothes. I'm missing lunch, dinner, all the good television programmes ... and my glass of wine! I'm also having to do this an awful lot once it gets dark, which has the added disadvantage of there being no light by which to see. We are a farm in the middle of nowhere, so there are no street lights, just the barn light, which is no help at all. Yuck, just stepped in another pothole I'd not spotted, and now I've got cold water in my welly again. Matt's no help: he's allergic to rain, I think, as even the dogs go out in it more readily than he does. He is very supportive when I come back in, though: impressed by my dedication, and handing me that glass of wine. Ahhh, that's better.

All of this foundation work I'm putting in now will make such a difference in the future, and not only because I shall stay nice and dry all evening! The horses learn to associate coming into the barn with when the weather is really bad: a behaviour primarily reinforced by some tasty food, and then the realisation that they are more comfortable when out of the elements. A natural progression from this point is that I don't go out to them as soon as I usually would when the weather is bad, giving them the opportunity to make the decision to come in for themselves.

To start with this is a bit hit and miss: sometimes they come in of their own accord, and I reward them with some hay and that lovely bucket of Speedi-Beet®; sometimes they are still out, but now, instead of having to walk all the way across the field to them, I can call them and they respond. The acid test, of course, is whether they have developed an awareness of self, and the realisation that the barn is more comfortable for them in such weather, rather than their action being a conditioned response to my presence. We shall see ...

CONFIDENCE = BALANCED MIND
Another of my first steps – I've lost count of how

A tale of two horses

many there are – involves confidence, or rather, a lack of it, which can be a real problem, and many behavioural cases I see involve confidence issues.

Many cats and dogs are doted on by their owners, and treated almost as a child might be. Raising children is done in the knowledge that they will one day be adults themselves, who will live their own lives, and no longer need us to provide for them. We know that our children must become sufficiently independent to go to school, and from an early age learn to do some things for themselves, so we develop and encourage the necessary abilities, and cross our fingers that they manage.

When we raise our puppies and kittens, we do so in the hope that they will be with us until their death at a good old age. Because our companion animals never develop true independence, and are always treated as reliant children, this is where the problem lies with so many of the confidence issues I deal with. What most owners don't realise is that, although their beloved animals remain dependent on them, they do not remain young: instead, growing up and becoming adult cats and dogs, but without the benefit of any of the psychological and emotional development necessary to behave as well-balanced adults.

The adult mind of all animals is very different to the young and immature mind. What we might tolerate as a youngster, for example, will often prove intolerable as an adult, and how the world is perceived is also different, as well as the sense of self. And, of course, there are many physical differences that occur as we age and become less mobile. If we do not develop our animals' confidence to enable them to rely on themselves and solve problems, behavioural difficulties are sometimes the result.

The same is true of our horses to a degree: although not regarded in quite the same way as cats and dogs often are, they do still need the psychological and emotional development just as much. For example, a horse who is not happy to hack on his own has trouble with his confidence: he does not have the ability to do things for himself, and

so is totally dependent on his owner, and although it's tempting to think that this gives him a sense of security – especially when accepted lore has it that our horse needs us to be his leader – this is actually not he case. A lack of confidence engenders non-specific anxiety, and even possibly fear and panic.

BEDROCK OF LEARNING

Building solid foundations – another first step – is vital; without these, our relationship with our horse is not sound, and will eventually give rise to problems. The correct way to construct a house, for example, is from the ground up, only laying the floor and building the rest of the house once the foundations are in place, providing the necessary solid base on which to build.

This is how behaviour works. If you don't put down foundations, whatever is built will crack and fall apart: maybe a couple of weeks down the line, and sometimes even two or three years.

But there's also another reason why this sometimes happens. Solid foundations are one thing, but it's also necessary to reinforce the behaviours we want our horse to use. A lot of the things we train our animals to do enable us to live with them in relative ease, but if we don't reinforce and reward these, it's no surprise if our animals become less enthusiastic about and not as skilled at doing them.

Matt and I have had firsthand experience of this, and it's surprising how quickly it can happen.

When we moved to our current location, going from a huge house to a tiny one was not the only problem we had. Arranging for everyone in a chain to move on the same day, and having the monies in place as well, is not an easy task, but if you want to move you have to put up with it. As happens often, our completion dates changed – and pretty much at the last minute – which meant that we sold our previous property three months before we purchased our current home, leaving us nowhere to live. Trying to find somewhere to stay in the interim was almost impossible: with five cats and two dogs, it was more likely we would be selected for the first flight to Mars than find a landlord willing to let us rent, and that was assuming we'd even get through the application process to get on an agent's books in the little time we had before we became homeless.

As our house sale loomed closer, and every agent told us there was no chance of renting with pets, and no time, in any case, we were out of ideas. What on earth were we going to do? Happily for us, rescue came in the shape of my brother, who very kindly said we could spend the three months with him, but that his house was not big enough for the cats *and* the dogs. My brother has a very nice house with nice furniture; lovely light-coloured carpets, and a well-kept garden with many young plants. Whilst he was working away at the time, he would be returning on certain days.

How to decide who, out of our menagerie, to keep with us and who to board? I thought about it long and hard. The cats were indoor felines, so would not go out and come in with muddy feet. The dogs would. Also, one of our dogs, Coco, was a rescue animal, and had significant problems with, well, just about everything, really. At home, we had a system which ensured she never came into contact with the cats or any visitors, but it would not be possible to implement this at my brother's house. She also liked to dig …

And so the decision was made that the dogs would have to go to kennels. It wasn't a nice decision to have to make: three months is a long time, after all, but there was no other option, and, despite my concerns, the dogs coped well. I was more upset than they were, I think, but I visited them regularly, and took them out for walks.

SLIPPING BACK

Finally moving into the farm, we were shocked at how rude and out of control our dogs had become. They went away well-mannered, calm and easygoing, and came back manic and unmanageable, not able to listen to anything, and barging at everything they wanted. Their change in behaviour was not really surprising. They went to a large, busy kennel, where they spent most of the time amusing themselves. No fault of the kennel, which was far too busy to maintain its charges' training, or wait until the dogs were all sitting nicely before putting down their food, and all of the other niceties that ensure dogs remain well-behaved and show self-restraint. A perfectly good place for a short stay, but less so for an extended one, and we would have found somewhere different for our dogs had we had more than two weeks' notice. After three months of minimum human contact, and no cues or reminders about how to behave, our animals reverted to type and became almost uncontrollable.

If solid training foundations have been taught, a situation such as this should not be too problematic. Reminding our dogs of the foundations learnt, remaining calm and waiting for them to respond, meant that, in a couple of weeks, we were almost back to normal (this also applies to routines, and not changing them to compensate when things go wrong if the routine is essentially good). I did not need to shout at my dogs, or try something different to get their co-operation: I simply needed to remind them of the routine, and not be impatient for change to happen overnight. Once their brains were back in gear, and their responses returned to normal, it all fell into place.

I've mentioned a lot of first steps in this book so far because there are many aspects to a solid foundation. Taking the time to build this properly is time well spent.

Chapter 13

Managing well

So far I've written a little about environment and a lot about behaviour, but there's a third aspect that contributes to a happy, well-balanced horse, and that is management.

How we manage our horse's life and environment – the choices we make about what we ask him to do in the ways he's employed; what we provide for him, and the various aids and equipment we use to help us with our management: all have an impact on how our horse feels and acts.

My view is that horses should be able to live to the best of their natural ability, allowing their bodies to work as nature intended. In the wild, horses are capable of living without us, but we have bred and developed the many different breeds of horse for various functions, a result of which is that some of their natural hardiness and particular abilities have been lost in the process.

Our objective should be to assist our animals in allowing their bodies to work to the best of their ability, and support them where weaknesses – perhaps due to breed, age, condition, or the environment – exist. There may not be a lot we can do about some of these, as we have to accept the restrictions of age and breed, but we can address all aspects of keeping a horse, and make changes to improve their health and happiness. Ultimately, this is what management is about.

Looking at management as being all of those aspects which have an effect on a horse, it's possible to see the interconnections, and how making changes in one area will benefit aspects of another

A good environment promotes emotional and physical health.

area, or compensate for things we cannot change. Evaluating each aspect will help us see what impact our decisions have on the overall situation.

CONDITION

Both the physical and emotional states of the horse are taken into account under this category. If a horse's physical condition is poor, his emotional state will suffer. His ability to cope with his environment, and perform in the disciplines he is asked to undertake, will be compromised. And if his physical condition does not take advantage of his breed strengths, the opportunity to develop his best abilities is missed.

If his emotional condition is poor, this will affect his physical condition, how he uses and expresses himself within his environment, and how he acts towards other horses and people.

ENVIRONMENT

This is taken to mean a horse's indoor area, his outdoor grazing area, and the weather. Yes, I did say the weather! We can't change the weather, of course, though we can change what we do to account for it.

If a horse's indoor or outdoor areas are poor, his emotional condition will suffer, and affect his physical condition in turn. The weather will do what it will, but if your horse's management rating is poor, the weather and its associated irritations and difficulties will exacerbate this..

BREED

This category has two aspects –

* physical characteristics
* emotional/ temperament characteristics

If we ignore what a horse's body has been bred to do, and use him in a discipline that he finds physically difficult, it may result in injury, and will affect his emotional condition, too: further affecting physical condition in turn, making him even less capable.

If we do not take into account his temperament, ie his breed focus, and ask for things that he is emotionally ill-equipped to handle, he will find this difficult. The result? Emotional distress, and/ or behaviours that are not what we want, as well as a negative impact on physical condition.

AGE

This is the one area that most of us try not to dwell on. Although we cannot do anything to halt the passage of time, we can do an awful lot about how age affects our horse.

Giving him an environment that he can't cope with will affect both his physical and emotional condition, and asking him to perform movements that are no longer easy or even possible will directly

affect his physical condition and wellbeing, as well as his emotional condition, further compromising physical condition.

DIET

This area is often overlooked, and not considered to have an impact on other aspects of a horse's life, or it is manipulated as a quick fix to alleviate problems instead of addressing the cause. What a horse eats – and how he eats it – actually makes a difference to many things.

If a horse is stabled and fed mainly on concentrates, he will finish his food fairly quickly. As he would naturally spend around 90 per cent of his day grazing, what will he do for the rest of the time, once his allocated feed has been eaten? The answer here is usually 'something else,' although this 'something else' can cause no end of problems.

Often the things our horses do to compensate for not being able to graze originate from significant emotional distress, and, as the situation that caused this doesn't change, the behaviours that our horses engage in as a substitute for the lack of grazing are never resolved. That such coping, or technically not coping, behaviours are termed 'self-rewarding,' is grossly misleading, as they are certainly not pleasurable activities. They never provide the compensation that the horse is seeking when engaging in them, and so continue indefinitely, because, for the horse, they are preferable to the alternative, which is to do nothing.

If medical problems ensue as a result of such coping behaviours, these will obviously affect the animal's physical condition, which then affects his abilities. All of these things impact his emotional mind, and unwanted behaviours in other areas of his life may then appear.

WORK

A horse's purpose in life – the job he does – is often overlooked. How many, I wonder, really assess their horse's strengths and weaknesses, and base what they ask him to do on these? Horses can do many different things, but, if taken too far outside

A tale of two horses

of what they are naturally capable of, there will be problems, expressed not only by his being difficult when worked with, but also in other handling situations. Stress will have a detrimental impact on his emotional health, which affects physical health in turn ... and his ability to do the work asked of him.

ENVIRONMENT – A HORSE AT PASTURE

Consider all of the elements that form part of your horse's life, and the effect they have on each other. For example, looking at the environment, and the aspect of pasture (a horse in a field eating grass as his main diet), the following categories may well come into play –

- Condition: gut health, physical health, emotional health
- Age: joints, temperature
- Breed: suitable forage
- Diet: emotional health, physical health, work, age
- Work: physical health, emotional health, diet, age, breed

Let's look at each category in turn, and what considerations might arise from choosing to keep a horse at pasture. Note that what type of pasture it is, and what condition this is in will determine whether the effect on each category is beneficial or detrimental.

CONDITION

What if ...
- *The field has a worm burden?* All animals may get worms at some point in their lives, and wormer is used to control these parasites. When worms are expelled from the horse in his faeces, they will stay on the field, and those that have not been killed by the wormer can remain there for quite some time, to be reingested by the horse as he grazes.

A horse's resultant poor gut health – which will affect both physical condition and emotional health – may also affect how he acts when being handled, or when saddled.

- *My field is more of a yard?* Condition will suffer if he doesn't get enough exercise, and emotional health will also be compromised.

- *The area is insecure?* Your horse will be constantly on the lookout for danger, compromising his emotional health, and, in turn, his condition. Should he reach and remain in a constant state of anxiety as a result, his response to handling and training will be adversely affected.

- *There is no worm burden in the field?* This will have a positive impact on the gut health of your horse, helping him maintain good condition and emotional health.

- *My field is large with room to exercise?* This will positively affect your horse's condition, which in turn affects his emotional health, both of which positively impact his ability to fight off infection and recover from injury.

- *The area is secure?* Your horse will benefit from improved emotional health because he is able to relax in his field, positively impacting condition and behaviour.

So, how best to deal with any negative features there might be?

A worm burden in the field can be dealt with by regular worm counts (a faeces sample is tested for worm eggs, which indicates whether or not it's necessary to worm the animal) to keep the worm burden in your horse under control. Additional measures are: remove droppings from the field (good practice, in any case); cross grazing with sheep (worms are species-specific); letting a field or area rest for a few months (without a host the worms die). The choice depends on area size and the situation, but each may have more than one effect: cross grazing with sheep, for example, directly combats worm population, and also improves pasture quality, as sheep will eat many of the weeds, allowing grass to come through.

If the field is very small, take your horse for regular hacks so that he can let off steam and have a good gallop, providing the exercise he is not able to get in his field. What else will this do? Improve your bond and relationship, certainly: getting enough exercise means he is less likely to be hyper and excitable, making handling easier and calmer for both of you. It will also make him less likely to present with behaviours which indicate he is not coping with his situation.

If your pasture has a good rating, great, in which case, all you need do is keep an eye on things so that it remains at that level.

AGE
What if ...
* *My horse is old, and the field he uses is large and hilly?* This may put extra strain on his joints, which then affects physical condition and emotional health. If the field is in an exposed area, he may suffer from the cold.

How to minimise these detrimental features?

Make sure your horse's resources are easy to get to, and that all of them are contained within a relatively small area of the field, so that he doesn't have to walk the length of it for shelter, say, and then back again for water or food. He does need to keep moving, but, perhaps, doesn't need to overdo things: your vet will guide you about how much exercise he should have to maintain movement, but not aggravate joints or other conditions. If your horse likes to be out but hasn't enough body fat to stay warm, buy him a couple of rugs of different thicknesses.

BREED
What if ...
* *My horse is a big eater, or is predisposed to laminitis?* A field of wonderful sweet grass is, perhaps, not ideal for some breeds, especially ponies, and weight gain can be a particular problem. Sugar and starch levels in the grass will adversely affect condition, which can have a negative impact

Strategies to manage grass intake must be carefully considered.

on hoof and gut health. Being overweight will also impact joint health and other systems in the body, all of which sparks a negative effect on condition and emotional health generally, thereby increasing your horse's chance of contracting laminitis.

Sweet grass is perhaps a more difficult problem, as most of things we do to combat this will have a negative impact on another area. Grazing muzzles will help, as long as your horse doesn't become frustrated at the rate he is able to eat. Strip grazing (a small area of field is sectioned off in turn to limit grazing) is popular, but greatly depletes available space for him to move about, run, and play. Allowing access to the field only at certain times is not ideal if he is normally stabled when not in the field, and can also result in a horse who learns to eat more quickly, possibly actually consuming more when restricted than when not.

So, what's to be done?

Are you able to have your horse on a yard with hay rather than in a stable, if he has only partial access to the field?

Can you teach him to eat hay as well as grass? It takes time and patience, but can be achieved. Grazing is not only a means of survival, but a rewarding pastime for your horse, which can mean he is single-minded about it. Other lifestyle areas with a poor rating (insufficient exercise, emotional distress, etc) may wholly or partly account for why he has chosen grazing as his main source of pleasure and positive reinforcement, allowing you to identify other improvements that could provide alternative distractions.

DIET
What if ...
*   *My pasture is sparse, or too wet and muddy to use at times?* What you choose to supplement his diet with will affect his emotional health, his condition, and his day-to-day behaviours, as some feeds will enhance certain behavioural abilities, making it difficult or even dangerous to work with your horse. Hoof and gut health will also be affected. Likewise, being unable to graze will have the same detrimental impact.

If, conversely, grass is plentiful and high in sugar, a serial grazer and those animals prone to laminitis will more than likely eat too much, and the problems noted in the previous section on breed will come into play.

Diet has an effect on all aspects of physical and emotional health, and many behaviours are directly attributable – in part or entirely – to diet.

And the solution?
By far the best thing you can do for your horse is have his diet professionally analysed and balanced, regardless of what he's currently eating. The best diet for a horse is to be at pasture and eating grass, although this still does not guarantee he will get the right minerals in the right quantities. Many problems – medical, condition, and behavioural – can result from a diet which is not balanced.

If your horse must be stabled, provide enough roughage in the form of hay or similar so that he has the opportunity to graze for long periods. Doubled-up hay nets make it more difficult for him to get at the hay, so he will spend longer grazing,

and are also good for those who tend to overeat. Be conscious of where you place this, though, and ensure it's in a position and at a height that is natural for a horse. and where they do not pose a danger to him (by getting caught up in it, say). Never leave your horse without food for more than six hours: a horse's digestive system is not designed to go long periods between meals as ours are, as inactivity can cause emotional and physical problems.

WORK
What if ...
*   *The field is small?*
*   *Very steep?*
*   *Provides limited forage?*
If a horse does not have room to exercise, his fitness will suffer, affecting condition, and emotional health in turn. Some breeds require a minimum level of fitness, even when not in work, and enforced inactivity will impose both physical and emotional stresses, affecting condition and how well or poorly a horse ages.

An unbalanced or inadequate diet will affect energy and resources, and the horse's ability to perform and do his job.

What can you do?
If your horse is unable to exercise in his field, provide him with enough ad hoc exercise to maintain correct condition for the work he does. It's not always necessary to take long hacks, as there are many activities (agility, groundwork training, etc) that your horse can enjoy in a limited area to keep his muscles and cardiovascular system in top condition.

It is important to support your working horse by providing him with a balanced diet, which should be standard practice for all horses, of course. Maintaining an adequate level of fitness and soundness to work will be impossible if he is not properly supported nutritionally.

You can apply the above process to every element of your horse's life to gauge how each affects the others. It's a very effective way of weighing up questions such as whether he would be better or worse off in a different yard, or, for example, the effects of changing a routine. Once you begin to work in this way you can make decisions that benefit your horse, by developing aspects that will make his life – and yours – much better.

WALKING THE WALK

I'd like my horses to go barefoot, as it's much healthier for their feet, and I can't think of a single reason to put shoes on them. The general consensus is that Thoroughbreds have rubbish feet, and will go lame if not shod. Using that information alone to decide whether or not Charlie and Star should go barefoot makes my decision little more than guesswork: I may as well toss a coin on it, as this constitutes only a small part of the information I need to make an informed judgement. There is far more to how strong and healthy a hoof is than simply the breed of horse. In order to determine whether or not Charlie and Star can go barefoot I need to also consider the state of their hooves, what can be done to get them in optimum condition, what activity they will be doing, and what surface they are on at home.

As it is, retired racehorses who are still on the yard tend to have their shoes taken off, and Charlie and Star were no exception, as they arrived barefoot, and my next job is to get their feet strong and healthy.

Some research tells me that there aren't many horses who truly benefit from being shod, although I am cognisant of the fact that there are many situations in which our horses require shoes to protect their hooves. As with most things, the matter is not black and white; neither am I suggesting that every horse should go barefoot. However, if it is something you wish to consider, be mindful that a lot can be done to make going from shod to barefoot an easy and successful transition for your horse.

So, diet, stress levels, exercise, and what our horses stand on at home will affect hoof health. If hooves are weak and soft, standing on a hard surface all day and night is not going to do them much good. They will harden, given time, but we

Tools to measure minerals.

need to help them along by providing different surfaces, and a yard and field is ideal as these have a combination of hard and soft surfaces.

Adding roughage and specific supplements to the diet in the form of balanced minerals will help hooves develop strength. I give hay ad lib throughout the year, and, when it's too hot in the summer, Charlie and Star stand in the barn and eat hay. They eat much more hay in winter than summer, obviously, but getting them used to eating it all year round has great benefits.

When analysing and balancing the diet, include foods fed each day that weigh 1lb (454g) or more, unless dealing with concentrates, in which case I would include those that weigh half-a-pound (227g) or more. The portion of Speedi-Beet® I give them is so small that this is not included in the daily total, otherwise, I'd be trying to work out the weight of every single thing they eat. How much bark do they take off the trees? What if they eat a couple of carrots as a treat?

The Speedi-Beet® serves several purposes: as a treat; a means of disguising medicines such as wormer; a means of providing minerals to balance their diet; a way of getting them to follow the bucket; to distract them, should there be a situation where I need to do so, and just because it is nice and they like it! Their diet is analysed and the relevant minerals to balance it are added to their daily portion of Speedi-Beet®.

Only undertaking the amount of exercise that

their feet can cope with is also necessary: exercise or standing on hard surfaces increases as the feet are able to cope with this. It's all common sense, really: if shoes are removed and the following week the horse is asked to hack for several miles on hard surfaces, his feet will be sore and he may go lame. If it's not possible to reduce the type of exercise he's doing, or change what he is standing on, boots are a very good option whilst the hooves become hardy.

The final requirement is someone who is very good at trimming your barefoot horse, as this is essential to hoof development. A horse's hooves are the equivalent of our nails; a reflection of our general health and condition. If we have a calcium deficiency white spots appear on our nails, and if a horse doesn't receive the right nutrients his hooves will be weak. In addition, the time of year and necessary changes in diet, exercise type, and physical condition all also affect hoof condition, reflected in their appearance and quality.

Knowing this is important. A horse's hooves do not look the same all the time, but this does not mean that he cannot cope without shoes. Hooves are growing and changing all the time, and the key, when trimming them, is to know how often to do so to encourage good health and solid growth, rather than leaving longer between trims, which may only allow them to maintain current condition.

My TOP MANAGEMENT TIPS
The following tips are some of the things I have found very useful and effective when managing my horses, and also handy when on a budget. They may not be right for you, of course, and it is vital that all medications and nutritional changes are checked with your vet before use.

- TEACH YOUR HORSE TO BE AWARE AND NOT TO 'ZONE OUT'

Will avoid constantly changing rugs for the conditions just in case he gets a bit wet, hot or cold without them; too hot or cold if he has on the wrong one. The other fantastic benefit of this is that his coat will start to grow for the season and weather conditions,

which means a lot less management for you, and less money spent on rugs.

- FEED FIBRE WITH NO ADDED MOLASSES, SUCH AS SPEEDI-BEET®, AS A TREAT

A really good incentive to come in, which also establishes a routine. Once your horse is in, put out some hay and pour the Speedi-Beet® on top, and soon enough he will be eating roughage (hay) of his own accord every day throughout the summer, rather than just that lovely sweet grass, which can be too much for some horses. What else will this do? Help maintain good hoof and gut health, for one thing: add extra nutritional elements to it, such as minerals. It will make medicines taste better, too. Oh, and it will also progress to him being keen to come in, eager for breakfast!

Be aware that adding or changing feed will have an impact on a horse's condition, energy and behaviour. Diets should be analysed and re-balanced to account for changes in feed, and your horse's level of activity, to ensure that the right nutrients in the right quantities are given.

- MINT, ANISEED, APPLE & LIQUORICE

These are flavours that many horses like the taste of, and adding some of this to your horse's bucket of feed will further mask any unpleasant flavours, such as wormer or some minerals, which can be unpalatable.

- VASELINE® TO COMBAT MUD, AND KEEP MIDGES OFF THE SKIN

This is great for keeping the lower part of the legs mud-free, and around here, I can tell you, it's very, very muddy.

I don't want to wash my horses' legs every day (it's not good for the oils in their skin to do this too frequently; nor is it something I or the horses want to happen every day), so, Charlie's and Star's legs get a good wash and dry, and I then apply a liberal amount of Vaseline®. It doesn't harm their skin, and will last for days before I have to wash, dry, and reapply.

Vaseline® is also really good to rub on the neck along the line of the mane and at the base of the tail to deter midges. Midges always seem to like the area where skin meets mane and tail hair, and this keeps them at bay without the use of harsh treatments that strip the skin of oils. Baby oil does much the same – flies won't land on greasy, oily skin. It's usually horses with sensitive skin who suffer most, so it makes no sense to me to put astringents on sensitive skin.

I might consider using this tip myself: the midges always get me at the hairline on my forehead, too!

●   GOLDEN UDDER™ CREAM
This tip was passed on to me, and is a brilliant treatment for minor cuts and scrapes. It is antiseptic and antibacterial, and allows the scrape to heal without infection, flies, or anything else getting in. When applied, the cream is cool and therefore calming (compared to other types of ointment which can sting) which makes life so much easier if further treatment is required, as there's no unpleasant association. It's a thick cream, and a good dollop stops minor bleeding, so you can easily see to wash and assess the injury. It is also excellent for fly bites, and those areas on a horse that are especially itchy and get over-scratched as a result.

●   ENCOURAGE BIRDS TO NEST IN THE STABLES
An excellent solution to reducing flies and supporting the bird population. The more you can do to encourage nature to maintain the balance, the easier it is for you.

●   STRIP CUT YOUR FIELD
Hmmm, given that doing this nearly killed us, I could suggest that, rather than strips, several *areas* be cut, which means the grass can be turned and gathered by a tractor. There will still be varying levels of sugar

A long mane keeps Star warm in the winter ... and her long tail is great for swatting flies in the summer!

and starch in the grass, which is very beneficial to your horse.

●   DON'T BATHE OR GROOM YOUR HORSE TOO OFTEN
Both of these deplete the natural oils that help keep the skin healthy, and flies away. After riding, horses can be washed down with water, and grooming confined to where the tack sits.

●   LET MANES AND TAILS GROW AS LONG AS POSSIBLE
Essential for helping to keep flies away, as a longer mane will cover more of the horse's neck, and a long tail has a further reach when used to swat flies. A long mane also helps retain heat in winter.

●   REMOVE DROPPINGS FROM THE STABLE
Sounds obvious, but, especially when the weather is hot and your horse is trying to get some shade by standing in his stable, droppings nearby will attract every fly from miles around. If I'm busy, I sometimes find it convenient to rake droppings into a pile at the side of the barn, and remove them later, but always remove them in summer.

A tale of two horses

- TAKE REGULAR WORM COUNTS

I get a worm count done every six months (as previously noted), but treat the horses only if there's a worm burden, and test again in six months' time. If the next test again shows no worm burden, this means that Charlie and Star will have gone a year without being wormed, which can be just a little too long, so I retest three months later rather than six, to pick up on any burden that is beginning to appear. If I have a second all-clear, I stick to three-monthly testing, until such time as it does become necessary to worm the horses, and then I return to six-monthly testing.

Tapeworms and other types of worm, such as bots, are not detected by analysing droppings, and require a blood sample or saliva test to be taken, which I do every six months a couple of weeks before they move fields. This way, if there is a worm burden it is dealt with in their current field, and not carried over to the new one.

- BABY BATH

A great product for bathing all our animals. It's kind to the skin, so is very good for those with sensitive skin, allergies or problems. It's very gentle, and doesn't sting if it gets into eyes. And you know what else? It smells lovely! I think dog shampoo is the worst: all the ones I've come across make dogs smell of wet dog: Baby Bath is much nicer!

- BABY OIL

I use this for getting serious tangles out of Star's mane. Charlie never has a tangle in his, even if I don't brush it, but Star gets dreadlocks if hers is left. And for those horses for whom regular grooming is not possible, this is a good way of dealing with matted hair with the minimum of discomfort. Once this is done, a commercial de-tangler and conditioner is great for maintenance.

As I keep Star and Charlie as natural as possible, I don't groom them if it's not necessary. I allow the mane and tail to grow, in which case, some tangling is inevitable. I have no intention of 'pulling' Star's mane, so having the right equipment to keep

on top of tangles without causing pain is essential. My childhood experiences of having my long hair brushed, and the pain of having hair pulled out by this, has convinced me that mane and tail pulling is not only unpleasant for the horse, but actually painful. It's no wonder that horses are not keen to have this done ...

Anyway, going back to this tip, the oil lubricates the hairs really well, so it's far easier to sort out serious tangles that may result when manes and tails have not been groomed for some time. A wash and condition will finish the job, and for those horses who can then be regularly groomed, the oil is not usually needed again.

- SET THINGS UP TO MAKE IT EASY FOR YOURSELF

When tools, tack, rugs, etc, are in the right place and easy to get to, it makes jobs much easier, and less frustrating. For example, the minerals I add to the horses' feed are in a plastic box, along with a note of the quantities for each horse, a set of miniature scales, a scoop, and a plastic cup to weigh them into, and is kept by the buckets and the Speedi-Beet®. In this way, everything is in one place, and it's a quick and easy matter to weigh out the minerals and add them to the feed.

When I have mucked out, the equipment used is returned to the stable, ready for the next time it is needed, which prevents the frustration of starting a job, only to find that I have to locate various tools before I can continue.

Keeping things tidy and in the right place makes life easier.

Chapter 14
So far, so good

It's the middle of October, and the year has been so wet that the summer field has finally given up. There is too much mud – and far too great a chance that Charlie and Star will slip and pull a muscle, or fall, so we are moving to the winter field about a month or so early.

I decided not to cut this field – and when I say 'decided' what I actually mean is there was no choice – as the wet weather meant that it hadn't grown well, so if I did cut it, there wouldn't be time for it to recover, providing hardly any grass for Charlie and Star, and quickly turning to mud under their feet.

The winter field is where they were housed when they first arrived, so no perimeter check is necessary this time when they get in it, just a lot of racing around, and then some specific hedge checking. Well, a horse needs to know who's on the other side ...

Charlie and Star last came in to eat Sunday afternoon, and it's now three days later. Although Star did come in for dinner Sunday night, had a mouthful and went straight back out, Charlie wouldn't come closer than the gate to the yard. Being out in the field is obviously where he wants to be, so he doesn't risk the field not being open when he goes back out, despite the fact that I don't close the gates and keep them in.

On the subject of routine, I haven't changed this, but after the horses were moved to the summer field earlier in the year, and didn't then come in for three days, I've not made up any Speedi-Beet® since they moved into the winter field. They are coming in

to drink, of course, but not staying. I reckon they just might be ready for some Speedi-Beet® this morning, however. Here goes: let's see if I'm going to just look silly shouting to myself, or if they pay attention and come in.

"Charlie, Star: breakfast!"

They've looked up at the sound of my call – a good start. I lift the buckets in the air so they can clearly see that I have breakfast, and ... aha! here they come, eating the food but going straight back out afterwards. Still, this is very good, and now they've done it a first time, they'll come in every morning ... and it won't be long before they're waiting for me to arrive!

Charlie's and Star's winter coats are really coming on now; they look like teddy bears, with hair three times the thickness of their summer coats. This is great news. Once again, accepted wisdom is that Thoroughbreds are unable to live out in the winter unless rugged up to their ears to prevent them dying of cold: another myth. Thoroughbreds are not naturally cold horses: their bodies metabolise very quickly, so they're actually quite warm, and, as long as they have enough to eat, do not generally suffer from the cold. In fact, for Thoroughbreds, being too hot is more of a problem; often they lose condition when rugged, as they become far too hot. If it's a struggle to keep weight on a Thoroughbred in the winter months, this could be the reason why.

AVOIDING OVER-MANAGEMENT
I don't want to keep my horses in rugs all year round,

A tale of two horses

Nice thick winter coats mean the horses don't need rugs.

and neither do I want to be frequently running out to the field putting on and taking off rugs as the weather changes, which is simply unnecessary, and a case of over-management. I am very pleased, therefore, that Charlie's and Star's coats are doing exactly what they should and thickening in order to protect them over the winter. Allowing their bodies to behave as they should, only putting on a rug if necessary, and not as a matter of course, or because I feel they will be better with one on, has achieved my objective.

In order for us to be confident that we are taking proper care of our horses and other animals, we need to feel that we are doing the best for them. Looking after our animals triggers our care emotional system; by doing things for them and making sure we have covered every eventuality our brains tell us they must be content, confirming we are doing our best. I'm sure most of us have left our horse without a rug in fine weather, only to feel worried and guilty all day when it rains, and we are not in a position to rectify the situation. This is a reasonable way to feel in winter, especially if our horse is old, very young,

or ill, or has no shelter and the weather is particularly inclement. However, feeling the same way in summer, when there's really no need to at all, shows that we find it very difficult to put aside emotional feelings in order to make a rational assessment of the situation.

Interrupting our desire to take action that will not benefit our horse but will appease our worries about him is quite hard, but can be done. If we can then increase our horse's awareness of how he is feeling in a given situation (is he cold/warm/tired/hungry?), he can decide for himself what he needs to do, and we can feel less anxious about him. It goes without saying that all the principles and suggestions I have outlined should be adjusted for each situation, so that you have something that works for you and your horse's lifestyle and environment.

You might be surprised to know that I see the sort of over-management I've described in connection with dogs, too; mostly when an owner is at home all day, and focuses more time and attention on their dog than is healthy for the relationship. The dog may display a number of behavioural issues as a result, ranging from an inability to do anything independently; constant attention-seeking; being over-excitable and disruptive, or displaying signs of becoming irritable, withdrawn, depressed or aggressive.

All of these behaviours and more are the result of an out-of-balance lifestyle, which causes a discontented and unbalanced emotional state. Owners take to extremes the care and consideration of their animal, constantly checking and analysing facial expressions and body language; coming to the (usually erroneous) conclusion that the dog is bored, must want to play, is depressed, sad, etc. In turn, feeling sorry for their dog, they attempt to make him feel better by increasing the amount of interaction, trying to entice the dog to do something all the time.

Some dogs in an over-managed situation display manic behaviour as described, whilst others become depressed or frustrated: definitely not the behaviour or emotional state of a happy, well balanced dog. That we over-care for our animals sometimes, and need to rein-in our emotions, is obvious.

Charlie and Star have greatly benefited from being taught to be aware; they can decide to go out into the field, and come back into the barn when the weather is bad. Being self-aware and able to make decisions about their own comfort has paid off, big-time, positively impacting on what I need to do for them, as well as their responses. Taking the matter of rugs as an example, by keeping themselves warm and dry, they obviate the need for me to rug them for every weather situation, which, in turn, saves me effort and money (even one each of a thick and thin rug are insufficient for all seasonal temperature variations). Charlie's and Star's bodies respond properly to every season variation and temperature change, and, hey presto! thick winter coats are coming along nicely.

Not wearing a rug all the time has the additional benefit that their skin is so much better when not constantly covered up: Charlie arrived with quite a few skin issues that have mostly disappeared now that his skin is healthier. Back in the spring, when the pair of them weren't in the best shape, and we had a couple of weeks of seriously cold winds, along with lashings of rain, they needed a little help, but neither has worn a rug, now, since April.

Go fly a kite!

On a lighter, non-horsey note, now that the windy weather is here, Matt has a taken up the hobby of kite flying. It's really windy today, and he's desperate to get in the field and see what he can do with his new kite, so off we go, him in charge, with me as his willing (?) assistant (someone has to stand with the kite and prevent the lines from tangling whilst he gets it off the ground, apparently). Out comes this giant, bright yellow kite with many lines attached to it. Hmmm, not much chance of me keeping this lot tangle-free!

Charlie and Star wander over to the fence to see what's going on, quite interested in this new, flappy thing ... well, until it flaps a little more, when they take a step back. Their curiosity gets the better of them, however, and they're back to see what's going on. Given half a chance, Charlie will check out the kite with his teeth, which won't please Matt!

Now for the moment of truth: will Matt's kite fly? Only one way to find out ...

Matt stands holding the handles whilst I walk backwards with the kite. The lines are so long, I'm nearly halfway across the field – if this thing gets into the air without them tangling it'll be a miracle! I hold the kite as high as I can so that it catches the wind ...

Some time later, after I've walked backwards across the field God knows how many times, and held the kite aloft as high as I can, I'm ready for a cup of tea. It appears that kite flying requires some skill, and lots of practice. One last go and then that's it for the day, I think. Charlie and Star have been fine whilst all this is going on: trotting up and down the hill, quite interested. I wasn't sure if they would spook at the flapping and the sound as the kite flew through the wind.

Packing the kite away I noticed that Charlie and Star had begun to prance, which soon turned

A tale of two horses

into play, and then progressed to them both having a good run. It was really nice to see them enjoying themselves, but then Star became spooked and began to panic, which made her instincts kick in, and she galloped as if her life depended on it. Charlie, bless him, did the opposite, slowing his pace in an effort to interrupt and calm Star, but she wasn't having any of it. Reaching the corner of the field Star slipped, but didn't fall, though this was enough of an interruption to allow her thinking brain to re-engage. Coming halfway across the field, she eventually stopped and calmed down.

The prancing, Star's ensuing panic, and subsequent calm was quite an interesting sequence of events, demonstrating how their emotional state can change very quickly. Breaking this down, we can understand that, firstly, there was no fear response to new stimuli – the kite – which was great, and could be due, in part, to the fact that I have deliberately chosen not to limit noise and movement in their environment, so they are quite used to things moving and making a noise as the wind blows. Keeping them in an environment where they witness different happenings – sudden movement from various objects, and hear an array of sounds – enables them to cope with these things. That's not to say, of course, that their environment should be so rife with noise, movement and things going on that they suffer sensory overload and are unable to cope.

Shifting emotions

So the kite itself did not cause any adverse response, and Charlie and Star were quite happy trailing us as we moved across the field, precipitating a playful mood where their emotional state was one of confidence and contentment. Observing their body language, I could see that they were definitely in play mode, and having a good time. However, as Star was running, she was getting faster and faster, and suddenly it was not play any more: she had shifted to instinct mode, using the fear system and the flight response. It's most likely that the action of her running faster and faster triggered the very familiar emotional state that used to occur when she was

racing. Star was unable to cope with racing – she didn't have the temperament for it – she panicked and therefore did not perform well. Having only been out of the racing environment for a relatively short period of time, it was all too easy for Star's brain to revert to the emotional feelings she associated with running as fast as possible (ie racing), which meant she did not calm down but remained up and excitable – possibly turning to mania, and also contributing to the fear instinct kicking in.

The shift from play to fear response is also often easily recognisable in dogs. I expect most of you have seen dogs having a really good rough and tumble which gets out of hand, and the dogs become aggressive. What is actually happening is that the confidence a dog feels in play is not sustainable, and a feeling of vulnerability replaces it, allowing the fear instinct to surface. Eventually, one of the dogs may begin to make the change from play to defending himself, or try to disengage from the interaction. A shift from play to fear happens with all mammals, including people and horses, due to a split-second change in perception for no apparent reason. Once this occurs, the interaction and situation become something else entirely.

In the situation we're discussing here, Charlie did not revert to instinct at all; his brain and thinking remained in rational mode. Although Star calmed down quite quickly after she'd stopped running, her brain was still in a state of flux, and it would have been completely the wrong time to try to interact with her, as the likelihood of her instincts taking over again was too high. Giving her a little time meant that Star's emotional state eventually settled, and it wasn't long before she was again munching grass, taking no notice at all of what was going on around her.

Developing personalities

It's so rewarding and good to see Charlie and Star develop, and to give their bodies the ability to behave in a natural way, with the result that they are so much more robust and content. Emotionally, they are coming on really well, too, with many small steps and the occasional big one, although they aren't always in tune with these. Star recently appeared to want affection from me, though didn't seem totally sure. She usually likes her own space, so this was quite out of character for Star, and made me unsure about whether or not I was reading the signs right – rather than wanting affection, she may have been thinking about nipping me instead! Deciding to wait and see rather than assume and get it wrong I came out of the stable: sure enough, a minute later, I got the cue I needed to accurately interpret her when she followed me out, asking for a nuzzle. Another small forward step in our relationship had been taken, since when Star has been quite easygoing, despite being in season this week.

Charlie has become quite the playful boy of late, and is showing a talent for picking up things with his teeth and moving them about. We have had rain and wind all day – not heavy rain, more of a drizzle, and it's still quite mild – and neither horse has had their rug on for a while, now that they understand to come into the barn if they feel cold, or it's wet. However, having been out all day in the drizzle, I thought it sensible to put on their lightweight rugs in case the wind got up during the night.

I called them into the barn, and, as usual, Star came in first and I began getting her rugged up. Taking one look at his rug, Charlie – who's not a fan of rugs – turned round and walked out again, with Star closely following before I'd actually done up her rug, so off it came. Oh well. I followed Star into the field, and she stood for her rug to be put on and done up. One down, one to go. Charlie let me put his rug on him and then walked off. Usually, he walks a few steps then stops to allow me to finish the job, but this time he shook his body and partially dislodged the rug, then gripped it with his teeth and pulled it off completely! I went to take it from him and he started a tug game so I let go, whereupon he dropped the rug on the ground and stamped his foot on it. Picking up the rug and holding it out to him, Charlie shook his head and did a little jump away from me, making it quite obvious that he did not want it on. It stayed off.

Horse sense

I am happy to be guided by the horses most of the time: I've taught them to be aware and to make their own choices, so if they don't want a rug on, then they're not cold. I don't make the mistake of believing that they always know best, however: if it is obvious that they need a rug, then on it goes, but if I'm not sure, I'll defer to them and check that they don't get cold. I've already said that Charlie generally prefers not to wear a rug, but something that happened about a month or so later let me know that even he thinks they have their uses.

It was late November and very windy, rainy and cold … winter was well on its way. The wind only occasionally blows from the east, but when it does it's freezing, with the promise of snow, ice and plummeting temperatures, and both Charlie and Star were a little cold. The open side of the barn faces east, so there's no shelter from the wind when it blows from this direction, so, on go the rugs. Very unusually, Charlie stood still for me to put on his, giving me a little purr once it was!

The next day it seemed the weather was picking up, so I thought I'd take off the rugs. Approaching Charlie first, I was surprised when he walked away from me: hmmm, that usually only happened when I wanted to put the rug on! What was going on in his head, I wondered? The same thing happened the second time, and on the third attempt he was out of the barn and into the field. Guess he wanted the rug to stay on? The weather that day eventually turned out to be as bad as the day before, so the rugs stayed on: ultimately a good decision on Charlie's part; he has definitely learnt to make a choice.

Every time I do something with the horses, or they respond to me, I analyse the response to ensure I am not creating a conditioned response rather than giving them the ability to make decisions. I must understand the motivation behind their behaviours if I am to go along this path of giving them autonomy. If I get it wrong and reinforce a response that I understand to be for one thing, when, in fact, the motivation is due to something else

A tale of two horses

entirely, I am likely to generate responses that I don't want, and will have the job of correcting these.

Of course, they are horses, but they are also individuals with consciousness and awareness of self, with a right to express natural behaviour, likes and dislikes, just as any other being does. It would be naive to overestimate what the equine brain is capable of understanding, which is why the study of animal behaviour should have a firm basis in neuroscience. I am assessing every step we take to ensure that I am not fooling myself, and expecting things that are not possible, but am instead seeing progression, development and understanding by my horses to the best of their ability.

TIME WITH MY HORSES

Christmas will soon be upon us, and work is winding down for me as my clients are busy getting ready for the holiday, which means I am more able to while away the days with Charlie and Star (don't tell Matt!). I should be turning my attention to updating my website, leaflets, and another round of marketing, but those can wait.

I love Christmas, and even more so if it snows. We have a lovely week off work to cook, walk, and potter about the house. Work on a farm doesn't stop for Christmas, of course: there are always jobs to be done, and we all still need feeding, but I don't have to turn on the computer!

This evening Star asked for more grooming, which was a surprise, as she's not one for being stroked. I've taken to giving both horses a little groom when I give them their last lot of hay before we go to bed. It's just so lovely to spend a few minutes with them last thing in the evening, although I must remember not to stay out too long. The last time I did so Matt came into the stable looking somewhat distressed as I'd been gone so long, and he was worried that I'd been stamped to death or something similar (he has a vivid imagination). It was very lovely of him, but completely unnecessary as far as I was concerned, as Charlie and Star are so calm and sweet-natured compared to when they arrived, and I wouldn't take any risks, anyway.

Anyway, Charlie had a groom as usual, and Star purred as I groomed her, which is not usual. When I stopped, she asked for more by turning her head to look at me, doing this three more times in total before she'd had enough. This was the first time she had actively asked me to continue with something after I'd stopped – brilliant! – and a lovely warm feeling to go to bed with.

Affection from Star: what a lovely end to the day! (Courtesy Andy Francis)

Chapter 15

Time to put my money where my mouth is

It's a bright, crisp morning, and I'm halfway through my advent calendar: behind today's window are elves. I haven't had an advent calendar for years; these days all you can find in the shops are cartoon versions or ones with chocolates in. Great for kids, I'm sure, but I like something a little more traditional. Having complained about this lack in my art class last month, one of my students bought me an advent calendar. It's brilliant – a proper calendar with detailed artwork of a Christmas tree, and traditional pictures inside the windows.

Walking into the barn, Star immediately approaches and pushes her nose into me. How very odd. She has become more comfortable lately, and likes a bit of attention now, but is this the same horse? She gently pushes me again, and turns her head, and then I see ... one of her eyes is swollen so badly she can't open it at all.

What I do next is going to make a difference to how this plays out, and I use the logical part of my brain to assess what to do. Straight away I know I need to call the vet. There's not much point me examining her eye, as I won't be able to do anything even if I can see what's wrong, and all I'm likely to do is make it hurt more, which means Star will be less likely to let the vet look at it.

I tell Star what a clever girl she is for showing me what's wrong, and that I'll sort it out. Although Star cannot understand my words, talking to her in this way will calm and reassure her, because my tone and body language are normal and matter of fact, letting her know there is nothing to worry about.

But I am actually very worried, and after leaving the barn I start to shake as I rush to call the vet.

In a fair number of cases that I work with, I see an animal's behaviour change quite rapidly once their owner is taken out of the equation. Animals pick so much up from our body language and tone of voice, and respond accordingly, so, without a nervous, anxious owner present, many do not have the fearful reaction they would do if their owner was there. Without knowing it, owners not only transmit their feelings of anxiety to their animal, but their actions often reinforce the resultant fearful behaviour from the animal, creating a vicious cycle that becomes more extreme each time.

The vet arrives and Star is sedated to allow him to properly open her damaged eye, and feel around to check for something in it. Thankfully, it seems Star may have knocked her eye when it was closed, as there are no foreign bodies, and no scratches or puncture wounds. In response to the trauma her pupil has contracted, and she has conjunctivitis. The vet cleans her eye, puts in drops, and leaves me with two lots of ointment and atropine, a muscle relaxant to dilate the pupil, which must be applied every hour until her pupil is fully dilated. The other drops are applied three times a day.

I am very nervous about the situation for two reasons. One: I hope Star's eye heals properly and doesn't leave her with problems. Two: what if all I've taught them so far only works when things are going well? What if, because I've taught the horses that they have a choice, Star decides not to let me apply her drops? What if my methods don't work when it really matters? What the hell am I going to do then? I'm sure the vet leaves thinking that I know what to do and am happy to do it. Well, I *do* know what to do – the vet was very good at showing me that – but I am very, very scared that I won't be able to get near Star's eye. And even if I can, my panicked mind asks, why on earth would she let me put drops in her eye three times a day for 7-10 days?

TESTING THE THEORY
So this will be the acid test for my belief that I am treating and training Charlie and Star in the right way, and not causing problems for myself. I can't predict how Star will react to having drops in her eye, and this uncertainty causes me to become anxious and doubt myself. But I get a grip and tell myself that my worries are unfounded. This situation is no different and certainly no more significant than any other I have come across whilst Charlie and Star have been with me. My knowledge is at the forefront of animal behaviour, backed up by scientifically proven research. I will approach this matter the same way that I always do.

But then another fear strikes me: if I can't get near Star to administer the drops, how can I possibly expect the vet to come out three times a day to do it? And Star has not been used to being tied up or physically restrained since she arrived here nearly a year ago … The hoof trimmer works with Star being free, and although Star has been gently led and held still for the occasional visit, my vet has mostly been happy to allow her freedom when working with her.

I call a halt on my imagination, which is working overtime. Having worked with a great many animals over the years, one thing I do know is that positive reinforcement makes everything much easier, not harder, and achieves amazing results. Although I have not put halter training in place yet, this really is no big deal, as the work done so far has set up the horses to be confident, and not panic in new situations. If I need to put headcollars on Charlie

and Star, they will respond to this in the same way they have everything else they've learnt: calmly and without anxiety. Besides, it's not as if they've never worn one, I just haven't found a need to work with them wearing one.

Well, I have to give Star her eyedrops, so here goes with the first dose of atropine.

I walk into the barn, put down some hay and talk to Star, then walk away. Okay, I'm not too anxious yet. Having been sedated earlier, Star is now ready to eat, so a snack of nice hay with all its positive associations is good, and I approach with the eyedrops. She is not at all sure, though, that she wants this strange object near her eye, and moves her head away every time it gets close. So go the next ten minutes, with me just showing her the tube, rubbing her neck, talking to her, and helping her cope. After a few attempts where I have one hand near her eye ready to open it, and she turns away, finally, finally, she holds still, and I squeeze a drop of atropine into her eye. Phew! I tell her she is a very clever girl, that it's all done, and off I go, breathing a huge sigh of relief once out of the barn, trying to stop my hands shaking – a reaction to the adrenaline that my body has produced because my mind seems to have made a big deal out of this. After just one more dose of atropine her pupil is dilated: just the other two ointments three times a day to do now …

I have not had to resort to putting a headcollar or lead rope on Star, there were no restraints; she has allowed me to do this of her own free will. But will she allow me to do it again? Often with things that are not very nice we become more reactive to them, not less, and I can't make her understand that she needs to keep still so that I can put drops in her eye which will make her eye better, even though it hurts now.

Well, so far so good; I've put two doses of ointment in today, with just one to go. I've been on my own all day, as Matt had gone to work before I did breakfast and saw Star's injured eye, so I've not had any help, and wouldn't have been able to manage on my own even using a headcollar, as I still wouldn't have had enough hands! When Matt gets

A tale of two horses

home, wondering how Star is and how I've got on, he is suitably impressed with Star's courage.

The next few days follow the same pattern with one small development. Instead of Star becoming more reactive as the days go by (which would be a fairly normal reaction), she actually becomes more receptive. Whereas it took me about ten minutes of gentle reassurance before she would stand with her head still, she is now doing so more quickly – within a couple of minutes. Time for a check-up from the vet, and it's my usual vet, Sarah, this time, as it's not an emergency.

Sarah is used to dealing with both Charlie and Star unrestrained, so we work like this today. Star stands and allows Sarah to look in her eye with the light, put dye in and look again, and administer the drops now due. Star truly *is* a star, and Sarah comments on how much of a big deal it was for Star to actually stand there and let her work on her eye, whilst being completely untethered and free to walk away. Star was calm, collected, and totally wonderful.

By the time we got to the last few days of her treatment, I was going into the barn, Star would keep her head steady, and I'd pop in the eyedrops: all done in about five seconds!

Whilst Star was having the atropine eyedrops (which dilate the pupil and prevent it contracting in response to light), going outside during the day was not possible, as there was a very good chance her eye could be permanently damaged by too much light entering it. Fortunately, it's wintertime and not exactly bright, so the barn is quite dark, but I decided that the only thing to do was shut the barn door to keep them in. However, before having a chance to do so, Star had walked over to the entrance, taken a look outside, then returned to stand in the darkest part of the barn.

Well, I have spent a year making them self-aware and able to manage their own comfort, but I didn't expect this. As work had stopped for Christmas and I was around, if I didn't need to shut

them in, I wouldn't, although I would obviously have to manage the situation during daylight hours to prevent her going outside and possibly damaging her eye. During the whole of her treatment, Star didn't even stand facing the outside, let alone go out, and Charlie stayed close, going outside for short periods only. Star did go out at night, but was back in again before it began to get light.

Throughout her treatment, I have shown Star that I am still the same, and nothing has changed with regard to how she is treated, as I did not force her to do anything, get cross or frustrated, shout at her, or make her do anything she was not ready to do. I am exactly the same as I have always been, and she has nothing to fear from me. A result of this, I feel, is that her attitude toward me has changed and we taken another trust-based step forward.

And speaking of trust, this is something we have with the farm animals already. Two or three of our ewes will follow me about, keen for attention, or curious about what I am doing when busy on the farm.

It is getting really cold and windy, and, although there's no snow yet, I'm sure it's on the way. The cows have a field shelter, but are still quite exposed. Norman is only six months old, and Ruby is still feeding him, so she doesn't have any excess fat to keep her warm. We keep the cows as naturally as we can, and as we have just three, and not three hundred, this is quite easy to do.

In December 2011 we were snowed in for a month, the cold trough that the farm sits in ensuring it stayed, once temperatures dropped (we read -26 on the thermometer). It was bitterly cold for weeks, but before the snow arrived, I had a brainwave: we'd put rugs on the cows! Finding a rug that was wide enough around the girth was not easy, but we did it. The fit was not perfect, as cows are not shaped like horses, of course, but they did the job. Seeing cows in the field tucked up in horse rugs obviously reinforced our neighbours' view that we weren't quite normal, but it made perfect sense to me: the cows

Our ewes are not easily spooked, and like to 'help' anyone who's about.

were warm, and still able to wander around the field instead of being shut in a barn for several months.

So, much to the neighbours' mirth, we've done the same this year, and, in fact, the cows have rugs on far more often than the horses, because, although the horses grow dense winter coats, the cows' coats do not grow thick enough to keep them warm when it gets really cold.

KNOWING HIS OWN STRENGTH

Back to the horses. I have been teaching Charlie to interact with me in a gentle way so that I stay safe and he has an understanding of his body, and how to use it in different situations. He likes a head rub: I rub his forehead and then he rubs against me. The problem is that his rubs are strong enough to knock me off my feet! It's not his fault – he's just being affectionate – but he's a big horse, and so much stronger than me. As well as this, he thrusts his head forward each time he rubs, so I get pushed backward.

The combination of strength and forward action of the movement could almost lift me off my feet and knock me back, which is not good, as he may inadvertently hurt me, and, if I am against a wall, it would not be possible to go backward, and

I would have to absorb all the force. So I need to teach Charlie how to gently rub against me, without moving his head forward and pushing me back.

The first step is to teach him how to begin this carefully, so that he learns to slow the movement. Every time he approaches me for a head rub, I tell him "Carefully," in a quiet, controlled voice and using body language to give both a visual (slow, careful movement) and auditory cue. Charlie has no idea what the word means at this stage, but my body language and change in my voice have an effect on his actions. This is not a new idea: if we talk loudly and excitedly, for example, our animals will respond with excitement, and if we talk quietly and slowly they will remain calm.

The next step is to show Charlie how strong his contact with me should be. As he rubs his head against me I stay where I am whilst the action is gentle, but move away as he becomes more enthusiastic and the action is more forceful. Soon enough he begins to understand what's required, and I have to move away less and less often to the point where I am simply adjusting my body a little if he gets too forceful, rather than stepping away from him. Charlie has successfully learnt not to push me, and also associated the word 'carefully' with touching gently. Head rubs are now so much nicer, safer, and truly lovely, and both of us really enjoy them.

That's not to say that he doesn't ever try to push with his nose: if he is feeling playful rather than affectionate he will do this; it's his way of letting me know whether he wants a head rub or is in the mood to play. As I have taught him to be careful with me, his pushes are much less forceful than they were, so there's no risk of me being knocked off my feet. How I respond also helps shape and reinforce the right behaviours, too. When he is in playful mood I move back a little so that the strength of the contact doesn't increase and remains gentle: there's no point trying to be affectionate with him when he's in this mood.

What Charlie learns from our playful interactions is that I understand him, and do not ask for things that he does not want to give, and so our

A tale of two horses

Charlie likes head rubs. I taught him to do this gently, so that I don't end up on the other side of the barn! (Courtesy Andy Francis)

relationship remains easy. He also learns that, in order to let me know what it is he wants, he just has to move his head in a pushing motion rather than a rub, without the need to increase the strength of his movement against me, thus reinforcing the careful behaviour he has learned. Most things I teach have many applications and crossovers, and this is no exception, as I can now apply the 'carefully' cue to

any situation where I need him to take care, such as when the ground is slippery, and I need him to tread carefully so that he doesn't slip, or if he is going past another animal who might be worried, or if going through a narrow gateway.

TRAINING: THE NEXT STAGE

Charlie and Star are by this time very different horses to when they arrived, and it's easy to see their developing personalities; their individual likes and dislikes. The freedom to express themselves and make choices affects how they behave – a situation that requires a different approach to the early stages of teaching. At the start, the stages were predictable: A plus B equals C. This is how we teach things, by repeating the same sequence until it has been learnt. Now they have progressed from this, their personalities and preferences come into play, and they are beginning to offer me variations in their responses rather than the same ones each time, which means I can now concentrate on refining and developing their behaviour rather than teaching it.

I don't need a textbook response at this stage; I need the horses to be able to interpret and apply behaviours to the situation they are in. If Charlie and Star can choose the appropriate response, or amend as necessary, then we are well on our way to a very rewarding and productive relationship.

So, how do we achieve this? Initially, by changing how I respond when they offer me a behaviour. Rather than working within the bounds of the same response each time, I now need to assess whether what they have offered helps us achieve our goal. In short, is it a progression, or a regression, and is it appropriate in this situation?

If we apply this strategy to all of our training now, we can begin to develop the strengths of each individual horse. If a horse is able to work in this way, we will soon learn what he is naturally good at, what he likes, which areas he needs a little guidance with, and what things he doesn't like. Knowing this, it's easy to put together a tailored programme for each horse you work with.

But how do we know when we've reached this stage in our horse's training?

Our horse could be offering different responses because –

• HE HAS NOT LEARNED THE BEHAVIOUR WELL ENOUGH TO BE CONSISTENT

If he doesn't know the behaviour well enough, continue to teach it until he does, applying these stages –

A If our horse performs the behaviour, he should be rewarded for doing so. When he is consistently getting it right, add in the voice cue as he performs the behaviour, so that he associates the word you are using with what he is doing, then reward.

B Once he has made that association, and understands that the word means that particular behaviour, say the word in advance of the behaviour. The word is now the prompt for our horse to perform the behaviour, which he should now do each time it is asked for. Go through the same steps for introducing hand signals.

• HE IS BORED

Everyone becomes bored if asked to repeat the same thing too often. Just because he knows a behaviour, it doesn't mean he is happy to repeat it endlessly. Keep training sessions short and varied, and add in some fun, or you will set up your horse to fail.

• HE DOESN'T LIKE THIS PARTICULAR BEHAVIOUR

Horses, like people, have likes and dislikes, and it may be that he simply does not like performing the behaviour being asked of him. Spotting this is relatively easy to do, as he usually knows the behaviour well, and will do it given enough positive motivation, or do it well the first couple of times, and then refuse. Decide whether it is essential that he is able to do it well, or if it is fine that he is inconsistent. If he must do it well, make it more rewarding for him to perform it, thus increasing his motivation.

• A BEHAVIOUR HAS BEEN ASKED FOR THAT IS OUT OF CONTEXT

Although our horse may know a behaviour, it does not mean that he can apply it to different contexts. When animals learn something new, they not only learn the movement that their body must make to perform the behaviour, they also associate everything else in a given situaiton with that movement. So, they will learn that their body must do x to achieve y, and this is done on the yard, in a particular headcollar, with this person wearing this jacket. If you remove or change any of these elements, it's possible our horse may not understand what we are asking for, as the elements necessary to let him know which behaviour to perform are not present.

Earlier, I spoke about the importance of practising a behaviour in different locations once it has been learned, and this is the reason why. A behaviour has not truly been learned until it can be performed in isolation – without the context and cues that were part of the initial learning process.

If your horse is struggling to do something that is familiar, because it is being asked for in a different situation/location, go back a stage and ask for an easier version of it, so that he understands which behaviour is required.

• HE IS OFFERING THE BEHAVIOUR IN A DIFFERENT CONTEXT TO THAT WHICH WAS TAUGHT

Great, your horse is using his brain and offering you a well established behaviour in a different context, to achieve a goal. "But my horse should do what I want, when I want," you may say. To some extent, yes. Obviously, you do not want an unmanageable horse who refuses to do anything you ask, but this rigid approach is somewhat flawed, and lacks any opportunity for development and progression. I want my horses to manage their own behaviour, and not be totally dependent on me, and I want them to be capable of thinking and making decisions. This is the next step in training, and it's essential for their emotional well-being and stability, safety and reliability.

A tale of two horses

I cannot achieve this if I only allow them to do what I want, when I want it, as this effectively shuts down their ability to think for themselves and make decisions.

The reason Star's eye injury was so easy to manage is because of this very concept. I haven't had a battle to treat her because she already has the ability and self-confidence to make an informed choice. Am I giving Star too much credit? Can she have this amount of awareness? She is, after all, a horse. True, but the proof of this is that, having spent nearly a year working towards this goal, I would say it is entirely possible to work at this level of understanding when teaching horses. Or dogs and cats, for that matter!

DAYDREAMING DOESN'T GET THE JOB DONE

Now it really is cold, and it never seems to stop raining – roll on the summer! Whilst I am not a summer person, it would be nice to be warm and dry instead of cold and soggy all the time. I have to change my trousers so often I'm running out of dry ones! As I'm mucking out, I think back to summer sunshine and a wonderful day spent riding in the Spanish hills ...

This must have been the first time I rode since those three months at a riding stable when I was eleven. Hmmm, I reckon I was around twelve when my brother, mum, her partner, and I went on holiday to Spain. I think it was the first time I had been abroad, too. I can't remember much about it, though two things really stick in my memory.

The first was a visit to Barcelona. I remember huge, impressive buildings that houses shopping stores, with so many different things in them. Also the fountains, walkways, open, airy spaces, all of which were busy, bustling, and very exciting. Nothing at all like Leicester City Centre, which was where we went if mum took us into town. And I remember riding. My mum organised it for me, but didn't come with us as she's scared of horses, and definitely wouldn't ride one. I remember my horse (probably a pony, given my age and size). Whatever he was, he was a light brown colour and very lovely. We rode into the mountains, following the guide for what seemed like hours, where I remember it being very beautiful and feeling completely happy. I don't recall much else, except when we returned we cantered along the beach to finish the ride, which was amazing.

I can just imagine it now: warm early evening sun, the spray of the sea and being carried along by a horse, the wind in my hair ... ahhh, too much daydreaming, better get back to mucking out ...

Chapter 16

A successful year

What a year it's been. It has finally sunk in that I actually do have horses: they're not a dream; they're really here – and here to stay.

At times, both ecstatically happy and terrified in tandem, I've learnt a lot this year, mostly about myself. I've heard it said that owning a horse teaches us who we really are, and this is certainly the case for me.

I've learnt that I have courage, and am stronger than I thought I was. I've always considered myself to be the kind of person who won't have a go at something for fear of failing or getting it wrong: the kid at school who never put up her hand to answer a question. What if I wasn't right? Would I look stupid? Would people laugh at me? Would they think I was an idiot? Even if I knew the answer I wouldn't speak out, for fear of being wrong. So much learning missed out on at school by not giving myself a chance: asking questions is key to understanding, but I could never do that, so what I couldn't find out for myself, or couldn't understand without help remained unknown. On my wedding day, I was so nervous that I had to ask the driver to do the route twice before I felt ready to go ahead: not because I was unsure about getting married – that was the best decision I ever made – but because I was shy and embarrassed at the thought of everyone looking at me.

But that was twenty years ago, and I have improved in this respect, and am much more assured than I used to be, although a lack of confidence is still something I sometimes struggle with. Part of me feels that it's taken all this time to get where I am now, and if only I'd done something about it before, I could have got where I am an awful lot sooner! Imagine what I might have done if only I'd been brave enough to try ...

Thankfully, in Charlie and Star I've found my courage.

Self-doubt is something most of us experience at times, and stepping out of our comfort zones is unknown and scary. If a negative response or feedback results from this, it's easy to convince ourselves that we were wrong to try. What if Charlie and Star suddenly become reactive, unmanageable, and begin behaving like wild animals? Immediate censure and condemnation of my ideals would be forthcoming, for sure ...

But when self-doubt such as this creeps in, it's vital to take a moment to question our perception, and ask: is it likely that this would happen? Why on earth *would* Charlie and Star behave like that? Behaviour happens for a reason; an underlying cause. And being sure that I am doing the right thing and not compromising my beliefs is more important to me than the fear of getting it wrong, which, in any case, is only discovering how *not* to do something, and trying a different approach. Keeping in mind my comments about being organised with a business plan; assessing strengths and weaknesses, and taking small steps to achieve goals, should help ensure that any wrong answers are only minor ones. Working with Charlie and Star I have found the courage to manage my fears, and go beyond my

A tale of two horses

comfort zone, rather than give up and walk away, and this attitude has spilled over into the rest of my life: believing I will be successful in what I do, and developing and expanding my life to be the best it can.

I have been with Charlie and Star as they have grown and developed. They have changed so much. The physical changes are impressive: gone is Charlie's skin condition and digestion problems; they both have really good, shiny coats (when they're not rolling around in the mud, that is); their feet are doing really well: a good shape, strong and hardy. Star has put on weight now she's no longer racing, and looks really well on it. Charlie has lost all the sagginess he had, and looks toned and strong. There is huge improvement in how they carry themselves; the shape of their bodies; their balance and self-awareness.

The scared, reactive horses who didn't know each other – or me – just a year ago, and who would rather run away or bite than be handled, have become happy, enthusiastic, and engaging. They play, investigate, and help us: well balanced, very happy horses who have a solid relationship with one another, and have given me their trust. And that they have done this of their own free will, because they want to, is just magical. Allowing and relying on me to look after them if they are ill, teach them new things, be a source of affection, and, of course, Speedi-Beet®, is something they have chosen to embrace. They have never been forced or coerced to do anything.

That old adage: 'The end justifies the means' is just an excuse to use abuse to get a result, without caring how such methods affect those they are used on. And using negative methods and pain

The difference in handsome Charlie now speaks for itself.

Star is thriving in her new environment – and looks stunning.

reinforcement will simply not provide the results that free will teaching does.

And that's a very pertinent point. Teaching is all about increasing an understanding of known things, and learning new ones; expanding knowledge and bestowing the ability to apply correct and appropriate responses to different scenarios and environments. Using a negative, aversive approach only produces a negative reaction, so does not achieve this.

Of course, there are times when specific actions without variation or personal interpretation are required from our animals – standing and waiting to cross a road, other actions to ensure safety, or specific movements in particular performance disciplines, or when working – which can also be taught via positive reinforcement. The particular beauty of working in this way is that the animal

is calmer, and more reliable should something not go right. Life happens, and we cannot predict each situation, so having a combination of specific behaviours, along with those that we encourage individual interpretation of, means we have so many tools at hand to regain control of a situation, should we need to.

Other benefits include –

SAFETY

Having a large repertoire of tools to choose from, with which to resolve potential problems, provides a much better chance of successfully averting dangerous situations, as well as increased levels of safety for horse and human.

RESPECT

Strictly speaking, animals do not understand the concept of respect: it is beyond their cognitive abilities. However, they do understand the practical applications of it, in that you can teach them to be careful around you. They have no idea that if they push against you with all their weight they will injure you: how can an animal understand what an injury is, and that it is the consequence of their action? An example of this is Indie's very waggy tail, which will clear a coffee table of its contents in one swift wag! Indie has no idea, of course, what results from this: all he knows is that he's wagged his tail. But it is possible to teach him not to wag his tail when he's next to the table, just as I have taught my horses not to walk through me, or push me with their heads when they want a rub.

AWARENESS AND SELF-EXPRESSION

An invaluable ability which boosts self-confidence, allowing a horse to cope in many different situations: solving problems, and finding better ways of doing things. It also enables great results when training, as the horse listens to cues and is happy to respond. It precludes the horse needing to use avoidance tactics, or being reluctant to comply, and reduces the possibility of behavioural issues. Physical and psychological health benefit, and, finally, it develops

A tale of two horses

the bond between us and our horse, creating a happy, content relationship.

ANIMATED PERSONALITIES

Providing the ability to achieve their potential through free will teaching really does create animated horses, who are happy and content, with the ability to express all their unique personality quirks. The resultant increased understanding of our horse – together with all of the other benefits – allows better and deeper communication between us.

DEVELOPING TRUST

A characteristic that runs throughout this book, which the dictionary defines as *confidence, assurance and reliance*. The work that's gone into building the relationship with Charlie and Star has been intended to give them the confidence to express themselves, and confidence in me and my support. They need the assurance that I will not be unpredictable, or cause them pain, or to feel scared: to feel safe enough to rely on me should they need to. And in return, I have confidence in them, and can rely on them to listen to my instructions and act on them, and be careful around me, ensuring my safety.

So what does this mean in reality? Well, happy and contented horses, for a start, who are able to demonstrate likes and dislikes, and develop their personalities. They have the confidence to behave naturally, and to express themselves in movement and voice. And they have an awareness and trust in me which is reflected in the care they take around me, happily moving their feet as I'm raking up manure in the stable, making the job quick and easy. They do not barge me for food, run away if I want to get them in, or exhibit any of the problems so often encountered when looking after horses. They don't use avoidance tactics or defensive behaviours because I have not given them any reason to develop or use these strategies.

The horse is a species that has been traditionally trained and handled using a combination of scientific fact, a lot of untrue or disproved

Trust between person and horse: priceless. (Courtesy Andy Francis)

information, incorrect assessment of body language and the reasons behind it, and aversive methods that incorporate punishment. Compared to this, using only scientifically-proven, positive-based methods and free will teaching is not at all the usual way of working with horses, even though these methods are now commonly used with dogs, cats, and other companion animals. As with any changes in tradition, it takes time for changes to filter through, and, sadly, there are those who still subscribe to the outdated and totally erroneous dominance theory in regard to dogs, for example, and consider physical force and punishment to be acceptable means of treating and training them. As the general public becomes aware of why this approach is totally wrong-headed, ineffective and morally corrupt, more owners will decide to work with those who treat their companions with compassion and respect, using positive methods, and working within the framework of scientifically-proven behaviour and learning theory.

Many opinions about the way I teach have been freely voiced, ranging from the assertion that I am idealistic, to completely mad to even consider working with horses in this positive, scientific way, but I was always very sure that there was no way I was going to harm these wonderful creatures, make them fear me, or cause pain by using punishment as a means to train them. For me, there is no compromise: there is only what is right and what is not. And because of this I have attracted interest in what I am doing, and received positive responses, comments, and questions about the methods I use, and how others can apply them to their own horses.

This first year has been incredibly successful. I've had doubts, but have learnt that, if I want to do something, all I need do is get on and do it. A few things did require a bit of thought about how best to apply them to horses, and the logistics of working with such a large animal meant that my approach had to be adapted at times. Some behavioural progressions, and some of my responses, also needed to change to account for the fact that a horse is a prey animal.

On the whole, though, these have been minor things. All mammals (including humans) learn in the same way, and once species specifics have been taken into account, well, it's simply a case of fine-tuning the details.

The results I – or, rather, the horses – have achieved are astonishing, and so many people have commented on the fact that Charlie and Star – with their calm, sweet natures and ease of handling and management – are not at all how they perceive Thoroughbreds to be. When I consider the many problems that other Thoroughbred owners have and then think about how flexible my situation is, I realise how very lucky I am.

Yes, I am very pleased (and a little relieved!) to say that it has, indeed, been a successful year.

Charlie and Star now happily eat in the same area; there's no longer any need for defensive behaviour.

Chapter 17
Look to the future

Being with Charlie and Star has been a joy, and I cannot imagine life without them: they bring so much happiness and contentment. This is what I was destined to do. Looking back on my life I can now see many instances where my love of horses influenced me: from my favourite fairground ride as a child (the carousel), to my decision to have cows on the farm. Cows? Cows remain my favourite amongst the livestock: their comparatively large size, shape and basic personality are indeed close to those of a horse.

I was not aware of any of this until Charlie and Star arrived, but I realise that this is what I've been waiting for all my life; this is the part that was missing. I didn't go into this with any agenda in mind; in fact, I didn't go into this at all – it was all Matt's doing! I have the horses I do because Matt thought they were right for me. He'd seen quite a lot of potential ones – and a few different breeds – but none was quite right. I had no idea he was off looking at horses the few months leading up to my birthday, and he managed to do it without alerting me that he was up to something! It is really important to choose the right horse for you, but I don't know what I would have chosen if it had been up to me, though I would have based my decision on set criteria, and not let emotion get in the way.

That's me being logical again, but I'm not sure this would have been the right thing to do, choosing an animal based purely on a checklist, and not taking into account how I felt. You need logic *and* emotion to make the right decision.

Obviously, if there's a particular equine discipline that you want to compete in, in order to progress to a certain level, your search should be focused on those breeds that are capable of achieving this, and known for their suitability for that particular discipline. If, however, you're happy to just 'have a go,' and remain at whatever level your horse is capable of, then this aspect is not as important. Many breeds are capable of doing a variety of things; it's how far you want to take it that makes the difference.

So choose with your heart and your head, and be prepared to be pleasantly surprised.

I hope you have found this book helpful, and will use what is relevant to your situation and your horse, putting into practice the techniques I use, adjusting and adapting them for your circumstances. Hopefully, this will also spark ideas of your own that will enhance and develop your working and/or personal relationship with your horse. How I work is not ground breaking in terms of training: my horses do not perform fancy tricks or complicated movements – I have not advanced them in any particular discipline – and it's possible that some would say, well, what's the big deal? My horse will stand still for this and that, and come in from the field when called. The difference, of course, is in how I've achieved these things, using only free will and positive reinforcement methods.

Using punishment, or aversive or negative techniques will never give the sparkle that comes from a horse who is able to express himself and behave on a free will basis. Of course, safety always comes first, and free will is not about leaving your horse to run wild, but changing yourself or the environment so that you can work in a positive and rewarding way without compromising safety.

Studies show that many behaviours associated with accidents and 'difficult' horses are induced by pain and fear. By taking these out of the equation, these 'problem' behaviours are often eliminated, resulting in a safer and more reliable horse, as with Charlie and Star, who are nothing like the typical Thoroughbred described at the beginning of the book. In fact, I'm not sure they ever were how I was led to expect. Breed traits do exist, of course, and are fairly reliable for well established breeds, but within a breed there are many variations, and sometimes a horse displays none of the characteristics typical of his breed.

One thing *is* certain, however, and that is that Charlie and Star were very reactive, and not at all receptive to being handled, but the way I have taught them and the interaction we have is why they've developed as they have. Had I done things differently, there would have been a different outcome. When training, we do have the power to influence behaviours, responses and perceptions, and with that comes the responsibility to ensure we do the very best for each and every animal, and assess how to develop them based on their individual merits.

Everyone can achieve similar fantastic results with positive reinforcement methods. Once you know how to go about it, it's easy to teach your horse to make his own decisions, to come to his own conclusions, ultimately gaining self-confidence and becoming autonomous in his responses.

My philosophy is to treat every animal with care and compassion, and use only positive reinforcement methods, and, in this regard, my guiding principles are –

- SAFETY FIRST

Safety should always be the primary concern. Working with any animal can be dangerous, so

A remarkable partnership develops when using positive reinforcement. (Courtesy Andy Francis)

identifying the risks and adjusting for them is the first objective. Working with horses at liberty, and allowing them the freedom to respond in a natural manner, can be dangerous if you do not first establish a safety plan.

For example, if unused to working with a horse at liberty, begin interactions behind a barrier, in case of unpredictable behaviour on the horse's part, and until you get to know one another better. If your horse is very nervous, excitable, or flighty, concentrate on balancing his mind and achieving reliability and calmness before working with him at close quarters.

A tale of two horses

- WORK TO YOU AND YOUR HORSE'S ABILITIES, AND ASSESS YOUR GOALS REALISTICALLY

You may have a horse who pulls you along when you bring him out of his stable. In his enthusiasm to reach his field, he may not care what he or you bump into on the way.

So, what would your perfect scenario be?

A horse who stands patiently to have his halter put on (point A), waits whilst you close the stable door, and walks calmly with you to his field, where you take off his halter and step away from him before he trots or canters away (point B).

There is always a way to achieve your goals with positive methods. You may not actually be at point A yet, if your horse does not like his halter being put on, or he may remain calm until you close the stable door. There are many steps involved in getting from the stable to the field in a calm and sensible manner, and dealing with these on an individual basis should allow you to achieve the result you want. It just takes patience.

What are your horse's strengths? What skills from other activities he performs can be used to help with your current sequence of steps? How can you encourage him to manage his own behaviour calmly? Does he like treats? Will he willingly follow a bucket? It may be that you need to clear obstacles from his journey to the field, and if he is too strong to hold on to, you may have to gradually work on teaching him to slow down rather than charge off.

- ALWAYS LEAVE AN ANIMAL BETTER OFF THAN WHEN YOU BEGAN INTERACTING WITH HIM

Remove anything from your horse's routine that may cause him concern, and then teach an alternative with which he is comfortable, and neither fearful or anxious about, leaving him in a better place than he was before. Not only will he have had an enjoyable experience, he will begin to develop trust in you.

Never work too quickly for his ability. If he needs time to think before he acts, give him that time. Always set yourselves up to succeed; don't worry if your horse does something different to what you require. Should this happen, show him again

what you would like. If he is doing well, decide whether or not to do a little more, or end there on a high note. If he does find something difficult, make it easier for him or find another way of doing it. Work with how your horse is on that particular day, and not with the expectation of what you have achieved previously, or what you would like to achieve now.

- DON'T COMPROMISE THE POSITIVE METHODS

Whatever you choose to do with your horse, work within a positive philosophy and its principles. If you don't know what to do, go and make a cup of tea, and think about how you might overcome the difficulties. If you feel yourself getting cross and frustrated, go and make another cup of tea! Your horse will thank you for it (and so will you). If you become really stuck, find out who else is working in this way, and ask for help.

- ABSOLUTELY NO PAIN OR INTIMIDATION

It is never necessary or right to hurt, frighten or intimidate an animal in order to train him. There is no justification for using techniques based on fear, or aversive/negative methods.

Remember your positive philosophy, and assess whether the method you currently use or are intending to use falls within its framework. Anything outside it should be discarded: decide upon a new strategy that does comply.

It may seem a little daunting to apply the principles I use to how you work with your own horse, and, indeed, some aspects may be logistically impossible. Continuing to work with and ride your horse, rather than going back to square one and doing nothing with him for a few months, is probably not an option, either, but there are ways of working through these issues and difficulties if we think outside the box.

It's not necessary to start from scratch, for example, if you decide which parts of this book will help you and your horse develop and progress. If I told all my clients that they had to start again and completely change everything they currently did

Fantastic results can be achieved with free will teaching and positive reinforcement.

the first you take brings you closer to your goal. Everyone has the ability to make changes, however big or small. Dare to dream ... then make it a reality.

Thinking about my own journey, I've been successful because I set myself up to succeed, and have found a way around every problem and stumbling block as a result. So much of what we do and how we are in life is based on our personalities, previous experience, and learned responses, and it's the same for our animals. I've spent a considerable amount of time making it possible for Charlie and Star to succeed, and we should do ourselves the same favour, especially when it comes to our side of the partnership with our animals.

Perhaps start by listing what might be required to realise your hopes and dreams.

- LIST ONE: APPROACH
Change to positive-based methods.
Work out better routines and management.
Work on a better relationship with your horse.
Develop the trust and friendship you have with him.

The end result of the last two points will be a true and rewarding partnership, horse and human, understanding each other's language, and working together. (Those with more than one horse will see better interaction and friendship between their animals.)

I'd like you to make two more lists: one about training, and the other concerning management/routines/how you do things.

- LIST TWO: TRAINING
Note down all of the exercises, movements, tricks, and clever things that you and your horse can do, and what level you're at when you do some training with him. Can he do these things occasionally, only in some situations, any time you ask, wherever you are?

Now write down how you can progress each item on your list. For example, your list might include –

with their horses, I'd probably not have too many clients! Even small adaptations can be beneficial. I started from scratch because I wanted to, and I had the time. There was no time pressure with regard to shows or competitions, either.

I didn't know my horses, and they didn't know me, when the arrived, but if you already own a horse, you will have an established relationship, so won't need to take the time I did getting to know him, although I might challenge you to take a good look at how you view your relationship now that you have read my book. Hopefully, you will have gained a fresh perspective and some good insight.

Are you contemplating your own journey? Are you inspired to try something new, aim higher, follow your dream?

Then go for it. If I can do it, so can you. Every dream is just a series of steps away, and

continued page 140

A tale of two horses

What do you want to achieve with your horse?
(Courtesy Andy Francis)

My girl and me – owning a horse is a magical experience.
(Courtesy Andy Francis)

A tale of two horses

☆ Great at backing
☆ Okay at leading
☆ Good at staying out of my space
☆ Really enjoys targeting

● LIST THREE: MANAGEMENT ROUTINE

Note down all of the management/routine work that you and your horse do. This might include -

Breakfast routine. My horse hears me prepare his breakfast, and is standing in the doorway when I arrive with the food. It's a bit of a struggle to get into the stable as he tries to eat the food as I am coming through the door.

Turn out routine. He stands calmly whilst I put on his headcollar and lead rope, but, as we begin walking to the field, he gets faster and faster, until I am only just hanging on, and trying to stop him pulling me over.

I spend a lot of time putting rugs on and taking them off.

Next, take a good look at your three lists, with the following in mind –

1 How does your current training list fit in with your dream, and what you want to achieve?

2 How does your current management and routine list fit in with your dream, and what you want to achieve?

3 What can you take from your training list and apply to your management list to improve it?

4 What can you take from your management list and apply to your training list to improve it?

Now think about what might be blocking the path to your dream, or sending you in a different direction.

5 Might you need to drop something from your training list to help you achieve your dream?

6 Might you need to drop something from your management list to help you achieve your dream?

And, conversely –

7 Might you need to add something to your training list to help you achieve your dream?

8 Might you need to add something to your management list to help you achieve your dream?

Giving very careful thought to these questions, and answering them fully and truthfully should provide you with some elements of the business plan that we covered earlier in the book.

Taking the second scenario in the management routine list, it is obvious that the horse has not been taught to stand in such a way that his food can be brought into the stable. But there is already a solution to this, as according to the training list, the horse is great at backing: therefore, the first item on the business plan would be to teach this horse a cue to move backwards when he hears his breakfast arriving.

Owning a horse is such a magical experience, and I have two wonderful horses who make me feel very lucky every single day. And it's not necessary to have pots of money to own a horse – Matt and I certainly do not have a lot to spend on them. Of course, if it's not possible to keep him at home, and paid livery is the only option, this will both increase expenses and limit choice about his environment.

I hope more than anything that my book will have inspired a renewed respect for our equine friends, and a desire to treat them as well as possible. There is no place for the outdated, ignorant, aversive methods that are still used today, and it's time we demanded better standards in equine training.

Every horse, person and situation is unique; what is right for one, may not be for another. Find your own path and see where it takes you ...

Epilogue

My life has changed far more than I thought it could, and I feel happy and relaxed. All the stress I had from doing too much, not wanting to let people down, and continuing with things I didn't want to do, has gone. My days are spent mostly on the farm, writing and working with clients. I have time to run the farm and home, and so much more time for Indie, Charlie and Star, which is the best thing about this. I am also starting to think about where I go next with Charlie and Star's development and training. There is so much we can do, but there's no rush. We'll take it steady, learn new things, and see what they enjoy.

I also have plans for a rather more grand and comprehensive business, using only positive reinforcement methods, offering rehabilitation, free will teaching courses for professionals, behaviour and management courses, and clicker training courses for horses and their carer. Whether you are an owner, handler, or run your own business, if you need a little guidance or an in-depth solution, get in touch (www.animalbehaviourist.net/). And, of course, I shall continue to work with dogs, cats and any other companion animal who needs my help.

Finally, I have learned that if I want to follow my dream and change my life then I need to get up and make it happen, no one else is going to do it for me. In years to come, when I am old and decrepit, I can sit in my chair reminiscing about my life and say I had a dream, I wanted to do this, but it didn't happen. Or, I can say I had a dream, and I went for it!

Our future? Well, I don't know where we will end up or how it will turn out, that part isn't written yet, but I do know we will enjoy every minute of getting there.

AFTERWORD
Unfortunately, in January 2015, our beloved Great Dane, Indie, peacefully passed away.

We were devastated: life lost colour without his happy face and waggy tail to greet us in the morning; no reason to go for a walk; no one to help us around the farm, or to share dinner with.

Indie will stay in our hearts forever, and our memories of him are of how happy he was, and all the things he did to make us smile.

Now, we share our home with Wolfie, an adorable Irish Wolfhound puppy, who is making us smile once more ...

Wolfie.

Index